A View from the Croft

A View from the Croft

Marina Dennis

Illustrated by
John Love

Colin Baxter Photography Ltd., Lanark, Scotland

First published in Great Britain in 1990 by
Colin Baxter Photography Ltd.,
Unit 2/3, Block 6,
Caldwellside Industrial Estate,
LANARK, ML11 6SR.

British Library Cataloguing in Publication Data
Dennis, Marina
A view from the croft.
1. Scotland, Highlands & Islands. Agricultural industries.
Crofting, history
338.634

ISBN 0-948661-17-8

Printed in Great Britain by
Butler & Tanner Ltd, Frome and London

To Aunt Bella – without whom I would not be a crofter.

A VIEW FROM THE CROFT

MAY

In the beginning — a rose

It is strange to think that Queen Victoria had a say in the view from my croft. It was my forebear's allegiance to the crown which secured for me the chance to view my world from the privileged position of a crofter.

James MacPherson was born in the parish of Abernethy in the early 1800s and volunteered under the kinship of Lord Seafield to fight for queen and country in the Crimean war. In recognition, and also by way of payment, many landowners granted the returning heroes a piece of ground, the rent of which was the barest minimum. But brave James MacPherson returned from the battlefield with only one arm; yet he proceeded to clear thirty-six acres of bog land on the edge of the ancient Caledonian pinewood of Abernethy. A far-seeing man, he first of all chose to build his house on a gravelly hillock looking south towards the Kincardine hills and the twin-peaked Meall a'Bhuachaille, the Shepherd's Hill.

He called it Inchdrein — the place of the thorns — or more aptly the place of the dog rose, still growing abundantly about the croft but no more vigorously or with a deeper blushing pink than by the old pigsty. The pigs have long gone, fat and squealing to slaughter. But it is here in this less than salubrious spot, by this victorious dog rose, that I feel closest to James MacPherson — did he also admire the falling pink petals or the vibrant orange hips against the intensity of a Strathspey winter?

So Inchdrein was built in 1856. One hundred and thirty years later I built a new house, a croft house, for the place was registered as a croft with the Crofters' Commission in 1955. But I had two arms to build it with as well as a husband and three strong 'adult' children. James MacPherson's house still stands and my view remains the same view he would have looked at, contentedly, I hope, most of the time, but I expect at other times, anxious and despondent. What would he have felt in 1863 when on St. Swithin's day there was a most intense frost? No doubt his potato shaws would have been in black ruin that morning.

April has gone now and good riddance to it for it can be a desperate month in upland places. The splendid weather enabled my cows and calves to be out all winter but the fields need resting after five months of hard grazing and very little growth. The hay has lasted well though and I still open the occasional bale which smells sweetly of summer vetches and clover. But on warm sunny days when I think spring has arrived, and the cows know it has, they gather belligerently by the gate, champing, roaring, butting – this low level rioting leads to a stampede when I open the gate to the forest and they devour a fresh pick as if they had been byre-bound all winter. Before long they are knee deep in cool bog water, munching moss-crop or bog cotton, the early shoots green and glossy.

Like most other folks my lambing was trouble free and I only lost one twin lamb out of twenty-five born here on the croft so far, and that was due to the sudden return of winter in mid-April. The ewe herself is old, a goodwill gift from the shepherds in Onich from whom I used to get my wintering hoggs. Her teeth are poor, worn down on the grey metamorphic rocks of Glencoe, and as a result her milk supply is inadequate. The kind weather when her twins were born gave them a good start, but the unexpected snow and frost was hard on the little one and he perished.

During that spell our jackdaws announced to one and all they were setting up home. One pair chose the tall chimney of the old Tulloch schoolhouse, the only house I can see in the view from my croft; the other pair built in James MacPherson's middle chimney. The frenetic behaviour of these argumentative, strutting, black-capped, grey-suited gentlemen reminds me of the dapper characters in a Chaplin movie. They flew to and fro, like whirling dervishes, with twigs and sheep wool and finally spent two days plucking hair from the cows' backs while they nonchalantly chewed the cud.

I watched as the jackdaws took samples from the beasts, finally settling the interior decoration of their nest by choosing the silver grey hair from Angie, the young heifer. As one scolded and goaded the other plucked, and strangely, when a beakful was gathered, the arrogant, I assume male, grabbed the hair and flew off triumphantly.

I have one cow the jackdaws completely ignored for she came out of the winter pretty hairless and obviously had a serious problem with dandruff, except in cattle it is called sarcoptic mange and is caused by a little mite. However, after a shampoo of the bovine equivalent of 'Head and Shoulders' she can now go anywhere without embarrassment.

I'm much enjoying my blooming auriculas (*Primula auricula*) which are one of our oldest cultivated plants which were brought to this country around 1570 by Flemish weavers. Originally from the mountainous areas of Europe, where they are called 'Bear's Ears', these beautiful primulas appear to me like paintings come to life with their porcelain-like flowers and velvety purple petals. I came by my auriculas in exchange for a dozen duck eggs for setting – it was a good bargain for the auriculas bloomed and the ducks hatched.

Warm fires – cold death

Old habits die hard, and thank goodness too. Here, as elsewhere in other rural communities, if you have more than enough for yourself, then you share what is left with your neighbour. So I wasn't surprised when I arrived home recently to find half a dozen blocks of sticky quick fir on my doorstep, the strong resinous smell hitting me as soon as I opened the car door. My neighbour on the hill had come across an old fir tree 'boiling with resin'; in other words, although the tree was dead, for some obscure reason it was still producing sap which was bubbling out of cracks and broken branches. Taking a sliver off with his pen knife he did a quick test to see if the wood would ignite readily with the flame of his lighter. It burned fiercely with a black, sooty smoke. As you can imagine too much 'rossit' as it is called hereabouts, can cause a real inferno when lighting your fire so you ca' canny with just two or three sticks of this precious kindling. I recall once having to buy firelighters and feeling I was somehow cheating and letting down my rural ancestry.

It had many other uses in days gone by and I remember an old fiddler who used to come to Inchdrein running his fiddle bow through a lump of rossit and going on to play a most sprightly *Reel of Tulloch* or a melodic *Music of Spey*. Shoemakers used it in the same way to make the sewing of leather easier and there was many a shinty stick given a longer life having been mended with hemp and rossit.

During the last century there were always one or two men in the parish who made a living out of selling quick fir or rossit. One such man was

Donald Cameron from Nethy Bridge, who travelled considerable distances on his horse to fairs, but unfortunately lost his life returning from Tomintoul on one such expedition. The fair there was called the Feill Fhuar, or Cold Market, for it was held on the Friday before Martinmas, the eleventh of November, and was a great gathering for all the neighbouring parishes. It was 1826, and business was brisk, but in the afternoon the sky darkened and snow fell gently at first, silent and sinister. But then there was a change; it fell quickly and thickly accompanied by gale force winds. The square cleared and people sought shelter where they could. The blizzard raged and there was much anxiety for those who had run for home and might be caught in the fierce blinding drift. Many died in the snowy wastes between Tomintoul and Nethy Bridge including Donald Cameron, who, battling against the tempest driven snow, laid the empty panniers which had earlier held the quick fir, on the ground, and sheltered between them. Both he and his horse were found dead together.

Eternal suppleness

My neighbour on the hill was inviting me to a pheasant shoot next winter when I queried his sanity and sobriety. The pheasant is rarer than osprey hereabouts. And anyway there are bigger and better dinners available for the same amount of powder and lead. He was joking, of course, and said it to illustrate the rarity of finding a pheasant's nest with twelve eggs. We both hoped that the fox, who is hard at work finding food for hungry, growing cubs, doesn't come across it for he preys heavily on other ground nesting birds such as capercaillie.

Talking of foxes, the old fellow here came to collect his rations the other afternoon as I was contemplating the view from the croft. The ducks were pottering around in the big ditch some two hundred yards from the house when there was a mighty commotion and the fox was seen to leave the disturbance with a white duck firmly gripped in his jaws. I let the collie out of the window but, by the time she had hurdled three barbed wire fences, the duck was probably being dismembered in the den.

There's a scruff of young starlings under the eaves of the old house keeping the parents fully occupied from dawn 'til dusk. While one collects yummy beetles from under dung heaps the other does toilet duty — removing from the nest the white faecal sacs and usually dropping them on my car. My twittering pair of swallows are back prospecting round the rafters in the old stable. They seem less exuberant and more subdued this year and I suppose could still be suffering a sort of jet lag after their long flight, especially as the weather now is colder than it was on Christmas day. However, perhaps there comes a time even in a swallow's life when the business of setting up home and producing a family becomes humdrum.

Talking of things which lose their appeal, I am definitely off nettles for the moment. I never minded nettles and would quite happily stand bare-legged in a nettle patch gathering juicy blackcurrants or gooseberries. I used to get stung but then I'd always heard that nettle stings were good for rheumatism so it was an easy case of mind over matter. After all, what was a slight skin irritation compared to a pot or two of deep purple blackcurrant jam and perhaps eternal suppleness. Well, the other day the mind over matter maxim was viciously reversed as I came in, literally red in the face, my skin screaming. You see, there's a hen nesting in an old milk churn in a boisterous nettle patch and because she's laying right at the end of the churn, which is on its side, I have to lie on my side, face in the nettles, and with a fully extended arm collect the eggs. I thought

13

about putting a stocking mask over my face but I believe these savage nettles could sting through Gortex. Anyway I'd probably meet somebody like the minister as I emerged and how do you convincingly explain that you are only collecting eggs. If I cut the nettles the hen will have lost her fortified nest. By the way, pious young women in Greece flagellate themselves with nettles during Holy Week as a reminder of Christ's suffering. I am a victim looking for a cause!

Tatties & bracken

The waters of the Sound of Raasay sparkled like a sea of sapphires in the fragile heat of this May afternoon. Alec Cameron and I sat on a bench at the end of his byre in Applecross and spoke about planting potatoes. An old man now of over eighty years, he had cut the toes out of his shoes for he had desperate corns.

We compared notes on our crofts – his on the Atlantic shoreline, in a warm moist climate but where hurricane and monsoon were not unknown. My own ground at eight hundred feet above sea-level where summers can be crinkling hot. Good times when you cut the hay and can almost hear it sizzling in the sun, drying sweetly and quickly; winter days with snowdrifts half way up the windows and the ground ringing like iron in the intense frost.

Despite being mechanically more advanced than Alec – we plough and drill my potatoes with a powerful and wilful Ford tractor – he could offer me some good advice to treble my crop. Alec still uses the 'cas chrom' or crooked spade to cultivate his ground because, as he says himself, 'it's quite as handy as anything else'. But that's not the secret; bracken is what you need and plenty of it.

Most of us would disagree wholeheartedly with that but if it's a full tattie pit you're after then respect the bracken. Alec used a little manure on the ground, then laid his seed potatoes on a bed of bracken which he says keeps a good supply of oxygen to the crop thus increasing it threefold. Unfortunately, or perhaps fortunately, for I find it hard to look at bracken with any admiration, we don't have any in my part of Strathspey so the potatoes are in cattle dung without the airy benefit of bracken.

JUNE

Her Majesty the Queen

Before the war there were two hundred colonies or hives of bees in the township of Tulloch; my great uncle had forty hives himself here at Inchdrein. Now there are only two. My neighbour on his high hill farm has one and I have the other.

Bees fascinate me and I love their caring, committed order of life. It's a complicated world, perhaps difficult for a new beekeeper to grasp especially if he were to read some of the old books with intriguing chapter headings like 'Bees – The Three Sexes'. Of course, there are not three sexes but three types of bee.

The most important member of the colony is Her Majesty the Queen Bee who is responsible for carrying on the race. Her task is simply to lay eggs of which she will lay up to three thousand in twenty-four hours each deposited in a separate cell.

The workers, who comprise the main body of the colony, are really undeveloped females and have nothing to do with the reproductive process, but ceaselessly tend the larvae, meticulously clean the hive and attend the queen. But their principle adult duty is to gather nectar and pollen while others make wax and build cells. So unsparingly do the workers perform these jobs that in a honey season they work themselves to death in just over a month. Their fragile wings become torn and at last an evening comes when they fail to get home before chilling nightfall.

But the lot of the drone, which is the male bee, is very different. He lives on the labour of others, does no work in the hive and gathers no nectar. In the bee world he has only one function to perform and that is the fertilisation of the queen. All through summer these big bees can be seen lazily buzzing near the hive; the workers allow them free access to food stores.

But there comes a day in autumn when a cruel fate swiftly descends on these luxurious idlers. With no more queens to be mated and stores required for winter, the colony, with some sort of inherited impulse, passes a sentence of death on the entire male population. The drones' one summer of life is over and they are driven mercilessly from the hive and left to perish from cold and starvation. Should a drone momentarily escape he is furiously set upon by the workers, his wings bitten off and his dying carcase carried to the hive entrance and cast forth.

I'm sure somewhere in that story there's a moral!

*   *   *   *

While out walking, my husband and I came across a plump little bank vole – a warm brown puff of fur, with bright beady eyes, mysteriously lying on the ground as if life had suddenly been withdrawn from it rather than death taken place. But like everything in nature if you look closely enough you will find the answer.

With the keen naturalist's eye, my husband noticed the vole was lying directly on top of a mole's exploratory tunnel which had just broken the surface. Some six feet along there was an entrance about the size of a golf ball. My husband made a squeaking noise rather like a rabbit being killed by a predator and in no time the answer to the mystery was staring us in the face. It was a weasel. We had obviously disturbed a hunting trip and now with the threat of losing his booty to another 'predator' the weasel swiftly dragged the vole down the mole's hole.

As I write there is fresh snow on the Shepherd's Hill, the north wind is grittily laden with chill showers and suddenly the lambs look much smaller. But lifting my spirits high above the dreich, sodden view from my croft is the boisterously evocative song of the stormcock – thank goodness for the mistle thrush.

Snap frosts, buttermilk and freckles

When Ian MacAskill said there would be frost in sheltered glens in the Highlands I knew that it really meant the ground would be white and sparkling when I got up in the morning. He was right and so was I. Mind you, that was five o'clock in the morning as I let out the collie who had a recognisable look on her face which said – 'I'm bursting'. She has been eating a lot between meals these days during this rabbit bonanza. As I stood on the doorstep, my bare legs gripped by the penetrating cold, I barely noticed the silver crystals carpeting the lawn or the still, sharp edge to the dawn. The countryside was immobilized in this steely grasp but I knew no matter how hard it clung it would be no match for the red-hot sun already sending out sunbeams of warmth and comfort.

Unfortunately the damage had been done to many tender young plants in the garden. In normal daytime I discovered all my tom thumbs had been reduced to a sorry, soggy mess. The tips of the potatoes were similarly affected and have since turned black. They will live to fight again unless there are even colder night frosts to come. Most badly affected, or perhaps what has affected me most of all, has been our struggling beech hedge which has not had a happy infancy and only just survived last year's drought and winter gales. The new leaves emerged a day or two before the frost and were obviously too delicate to withstand that icy grip. They are black and shrivelled – my hedge, once full of tender young promise, is now nothing more than a line of brown twigs stuck in the ground.

Carl Von Linne or Linnaeus, the Swedish father of botany, was also familiar with these treacherous, silent night frosts. In a little flower calendar of his which I often read he explains that these frosts come from north of the Arctic circle and that there are three categories of frost. The first is the lead cold arising from the thaws in Lapmark and happens at the end of the leafing season, May 9th – May 25th. This leaden frost was obviously what destroyed my beeches. Then comes the brass cold from the snow melting in Lapland at the beginning of the fruiting season, June 20th – July 12th. The iron cold comes from the freezing on the Lapland Alps in the middle of sowing time or seeding time, August 28th – September 22nd. Linnaeus writes that these frosts do not happen at the same time as they do in Lapland but arrive some eight days later. He adds that the leaden nights happen before the leafing of the ash and while the ash is leafing there will be no more frosts until it is fully in leaf. Another of his calendar sayings is that while the cuckoo flower blooms the salmon go up the rivers and dragonflies come forth. Last Saturday I saw my first dragonfly hovering over a murky, glassy pool in a forest clearing.

Staying with Swedish thinking, the idea of having a veranda on our croft house came as a result of having a holiday in that country. There, in summertime, all meals are eaten outside on their wooden verandas. With the delicious heat last weekend, and having friends staying, we all ate and drank in the view from the croft amongst other things. A younger member of our party was concerned about the sun highlighting her freckles and wondered how she could disguise them. I think freckles are very attractive but I told her of the old trick of washing your face in buttermilk which was said to fade freckles and also bring relief from sunburn. Certainly much cheaper than the ultra-expensive, ultra-violet sun blockers and after-sun lotions widely available, but unfortunately, extremely difficult to come by nowadays. Most natural lotions recommended for fading unwanted freckles have the same effect on age spots. What I want to know is at what age do attractive freckles become embarrassing age spots?

*   *   *   *

Apart from rowans, I see no flowering trees in the view from my croft but recently while walking near Loch-an-eilean I was surrounded by brocades of blossom on a variety of trees. Most impressive were several splendid lime trees – a summer home of murmurous wings– as Tennyson wrote. To stand beneath a lime tree on a warm May day with the soporific hum of myriads of bees and the air heavy with the exquisite perfume of lime flowers is a peaceful if not nostalgic experience reminiscent of lazy, hazy less fraught times. Surprisingly the lime tree is not the correct name for this tree and bears no resemblance to that cousin of the orange and lemon trees and, of course, produces no limes. The proper name for the lime tree as we know it is the linden or line tree. The name line is derived from the once valuable inner bark of the tree which, when stripped, comes off in long string like pieces or lines resembling dried grass. Gardeners used this line to secure delicate plants from wind damage and to tie up bunches of flowers.

The musky trail of the fox

Despite the fierce and continuous war waged against the fox in most places it manages to hold its own and is arrogant and proud of the fact.

Here at Inchdrein an uneasy peace reigns with Master Reynard. He doesn't know it but I have a sneaking admiration for him and enjoy nothing better than observing him silently pad the musky trail of his territory. He is elegant and bold, sensitive and delicate as he comes across a new scent on his patch. But there is no doubt that the fox is the most unequivocally hated animal in the Highlands. Persistently persecuted in the spring with gun, snares and trap and the dens and cubs are marauded by terriers. Yet it was not always so. Around the beginning of the eighteenth century Duncan Ban MacIntyre, the great Gaelic poet wrote his 'Oram nam Balgairean' – the Song of the Foxes. It was really a personal comment on the coming of sheep to the Highlands and he was held in high regard by fellow kinsmen as a result.

> My blessing be upon the foxes, for that
> they hunt the sheep –
> The sheep with the brockit faces that have
> made confusion in all the world,
> Turning our country to desert and putting
> up the rents of our lands.

He ends by wishing good luck to all the foxes and that they may never die but of old age.

Well, I think the fox here has had more than his fair share of Duncan Ban MacIntyre's good luck. We have one den, I know not where, nor do I look for it so that, when my neighbours ask, I can truthfully say I've no idea where the foxes are. But I have to admit that full scale war almost broke out the other day as we sat at breakfast watching the fox patrol the forest edge a few yards from the lambing park. His confident, right-to-be-there attitude rankled more than a bit. He was breaking the rules of the peace agreement – no lambs, maybe the odd teuch Rhode Island Red or rangey, stravaiging drake, but absolutely no lambs. He was definitely in no man's land now and reserve gunfire was summoned. A few ear-splitting shots over his head terrified the ewes and only made his ears twitch. Obviously he thought there was no need to retreat with such a hopelessly inaccurate rifleman. We had to gain the upper hand and quick, so my husband took the collie, advanced on the enemy, and gave instructions. The dog took off, the fox assessed the situation and in a split second was away. Nell chased him over bog-myrtle and blaeberry, through juniper and pinewood only letting him go as he jumped the burn between the lochs, almost a mile from the confrontation. I am sure he will be back in his haunts by now metaphorically licking his wounds.

I have to admit to belonging to that rather sedentary and not very adventurous group of birdwatchers who really only watch birds in their garden although in my case it's my croft. Nevertheless, I get enormous pleasure from doing so and this week has been a five star occasion. No, I don't have a red-flanked blue-tail on my croft but a wonderful pair of lapwings! I can hardly take my eyes off them for it's the first time in nearly a decade that they have nested at Inchdrein. They are beautiful, evocative birds. In the last few days the handsomely groomed crested male has been courting an almost disinterested hen – how can she resist that husky, seductive, plaintive call? It says everything to her in an emotional cadence of sound. And he's doing everything possible to please her. Their home is to be an elevated clump of rushes in a marshy plot – 'breac le neoineanaibh' – chequered with daisies. Today she is sitting attending to her brood patch but is still rather high in the nest yet to have a full clutch of eggs. Already they have refined a most ludicrous but successful distraction display to lead away silly, brainless hoggs from the nest site.

Summer sun and warmth are here – a thick, furry bumble bee buzzes by on gossamer wings to plunder my fat peonies.

The legless table

Every year, at this time, I become obsessed with the patch of snow in the gloomy northern corrie of the Shepherd's Hill. Will it break the record by remaining there until the 24th of June as in 1986? But the grimy snow is dwindling daily and before long the bumpy bald mass of the Kincardine hills will be naked brown, waiting to be clad in flushing green for summer and soft purple for autumn. On the other side of my mountain the scene is different and harsher as the snow clings at higher altitude. However, without any real snow until mid-February, I doubt whether there will be any permanent snowfields on Cairngorm this year. Having said that, though, a friend who works for the Cairngorm Chairlift Company tells me that the great snow wreath on Cairngorm called the 'Cuidhe Crom' or the crooked wreath is still intact.

I am always glad to see the last of the snow go but there were a few occasions this winter when a skiff of snow would have solved some puzzles. The first problem concerned sheep. You would have thought that twenty hoggs might have been content grazing eight hundred acres of moorland along with good shelter and a dry bed. Whether they turned tail and made for my neighbour's fields as soon as I left them, I know not. Certainly three days later along with a day traipsing through ankle-breaking bogs produced no sighting of the beasts. Had there been a light fall of snow their escape would have been noticed, their route followed and location exposed in no more than an hour. So you see snow can occasionally simplify life and also help solve the mysteries of our natural world. This was no more evident than some weeks back when my neighbour on the hill was most disturbed by an unseen force performing what he reckoned was an impossible task. He had shot a marauding deer, and after skinning and butchering the beast in his barn, he left the lower portions of the four legs on a table to dispose of next day. However, in the morning there were only three legs left. He knew the barn was completely secure from cats and dogs and he had no rats. Intrigued, he left the three legs overnight, and as they say, lo and behold, there were only two legs left in the morning. It bothered him greatly and he spent some considerable time checking for recently excavated tunnels where perhaps a pine marten might be at work. But there was still no trace of the mysterious leg remover. You've probably guessed that the third leg was gone the following morning. He came almost begging me to join in communal prayer for a fall of snow to solve the puzzle of the limb predator. He obviously was not impressed by my pleas to the weather gods because he decided that, rather than lose the fourth leg with the mystery still unsolved, he would remove the leg and replace it when there was snow cover. Snow fell. It worked a treat — the legless table was there in the morning and so, too, a track in the snow of tiny delicate footprints, easily identified as that of a stoat. Under the barn door was a tiny space caused by the uneven ground, just big enough to allow the stoat to pull the deer's leg through, but with a struggle. It was all so obvious in the snow.

I am always sorry in one way to see the swifts and flycatchers arrive for they are the last of our summer visitors. By the time they get here a whole range of birds have already hatched, from golden eagle to oyster-catcher, starling to wren. The swift, the Latin name of which means the martin without feet, is also known in some areas as 'Jack Screamer'. They rarely use their tiny feet, spending most of their time in impetuous flight careering around the skies screaming shrilly. Their bill appears equally tiny at first glance but, when opened, has a huge gape which enables them to fill a pouch under their tongue with insects with which they feed their young. Because they are late nesters, swifts are still displaying, their aerial antics quite spectacular. One pair of not quite so aerobatically-able swifts landed on a friend's lawn recently in a dusky bundle of high-pitched squeaks. They were two males, presumably, who had wrongly assumed that the sky was the limit, flew higher and higher, egging each other on, grasped claws, and then, inextricably bound to each other and more or less flightless, fell ignominiously to earth with a thump. They were so tightly tangled together, blood was drawn in the struggle to separate the birds. Eventually the warriors, once more airborne, flew past screaming abuse at each other.

The last crop of all to be sown on the croft is always swede and this year I am trying a new system whereby I don't have the swedes growing in drills but at a higher density in a flat field. As a result the swedes will be smaller but there should be more of them – hopefully! I have gone for a leafy variety which should be ideal for strip feeding in the winter. But it is a real trauchle discing and harrowing the ground to a fine tilth. However, the discing was made easier this year after inheriting a fine set of disc harrows from my neighbour on the hill, who bought them for a song after the war. They were originally manufactured in Australia, bought by the Department of Agriculture who used them during the war to help farmers increase production. That system was discontinued after the war and much first rate machinery was disposed of. Despite the fifty year gap the Sunshine disc harrows, as they are called, most efficiently chewed up and destroyed the tangled clods of couch grass, which is more than can be said for a set of harrows I once saw being used in the Ebro delta in eastern Spain. On one side of the road there was a farmer harrowing his land with a donkey pulling a large spikey branch through the ground; on the other side of the road there were three huge tractors grading the ground with laser precision harrows. At the time, I suppose I thought the man with the donkey quaint but further travels in rural Spain persuaded me that, in fact, it was common. So you will understand why I glow with pride at my Sunshine harrows.

Displenish sales and the wrath of God

Despite modern communications with signals being beamed and bounced off satellites in space, there is nothing quite like a farm displenish sale to spread news quickly. For example, I found out from a friend who was at the auction that I had bought a Massey Ferguson hay baler before I knew I had bought it myself. I was away looking at Highland ponies in Glen Feshie and couldn't get to the sale so I had asked a reliably 'spirit-less' neighbour to bid on the baler for me. He successfully secured the baler but a few folk wondered what a 'big farmer' like him was doing buying a piddling little square baler with which it would take him, with his acreage, from now 'til harvest to bale his hay! So most folk knew my business before I did – but I also found out who had bought the snowplough, the old grey Fergie tractor and the antique turnip sower; and the wise wives who took the cars away from sociable spouses!

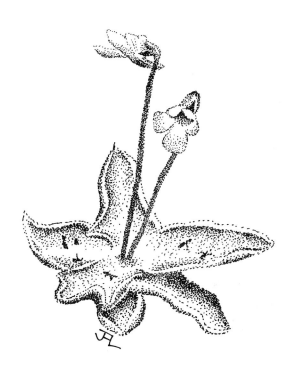

How well my cattle look on their summer grazing, black and shiny as if I had been out with Cherry Blossom and brush. They have settled quickly, neither testing fences or bawling for home – grass, shade, shelter and water are working wonders. At twelve hundred feet above sea level, with a cool breeze off the Shepherd's Hill there are few flies to pester them. But it is a grand excuse for me to go stravaiging through new territory – there is a mass of moorland and marsh flowers to identify and admire. The straggly-coated blackface sheep have gone to loftier pastures for a short time until the clipping comes round and a host of plants flower. The speed at which they grow and bloom amazes me, this headlong rush to flower and seed, to catch the ripening sun, to soak up the soft summer rain. I walked past a dreary patch of mossy ground earlier in the week, no glimmer of light or colour apparent; next afternoon life had erupted in crisp new shades from the dazzling purple of butterwort, the blushing rose of louse wort to the fragile pink of spotted orchid. Around the bog edges, brave and open faced, grew the delicate chickweed wintergreen. Butterwort is also known as the bog-violet and in Gaelic as mothan, although the word also means yirning or earning grass which acts like rennet on cow's milk, turning it to curds. Tradition has it that if a young man makes a miraculous escape (I'm not sure whether this refers to a dangerous situation or an ensnaring woman) it is said of him – Dh'ol e bainne na bo ba a dh'ith am mothan – he drank the milk of the guileless cow that ate the mothan. I wonder if the pasteurisation of milk nowadays destroys the magical effect of the mothan! For the sake of our young men it is to be hoped that there are enough guileless cows about to save their bacon! It was also considered a love potion: the woman giving it goes down on her left knee and plucks nine roots of butterwort, knots them together to make a ring which is then placed on the mouth of the girl to make the man she kisses her slave for life! It was also considered wise to place butterwort under a woman giving birth to ensure safe delivery, and for travellers to carry some to protect them on their journeys.

*   *   *   *

We are halfway through the year and the aspen tree is only now bursting into leaf. Until recently their naked pale branches stood like skeletons among the vibrancy of blossom and leaf of the rowans and birches. The aspen, a member of the poplar family, is a very special tree here in the highlands and grows abundantly. It is easy to identify for the leaves are never still, they tremble and quiver incessantly and you can always hear the gentle rustle of one against the other. I have often heard it told in this area the reason the aspen trembles is because at the Crucifixion the cross of Christ was made of aspen and the tree always shudders at the recollection of the cruel purpose it served. My old friend with the lump of rossit in his fiddle case had great respect for aspens. He was very fond of a dram and on his way home after a few too many would always stagger smartly past the aspen trees for he felt that it was better to face the wrath of his old mother than fall beneath the aspens and face the wrath of God!

JULY

The death of a croft

The road was made by cart rather than man and wound this way and that more to please itself, it seemed. It took you unawares at times so that your next footstep was in the wrong direction; a pleasant surprise this contrary track. No sign post said there is a ford round the corner; thank goodness. There was no warning about the road narrowing due to pavements of bulging yellow broom; thank goodness. There was no diversion signs at the arthritic, grey, scaly birch tree, across the road; thank goodness. And there was nothing to say that once you crossed the ford, that was the end of the road.

Directly in front of me was a high grassy hillock over which I could see nothing except, away in the distance, the high velvety brown shoulders of Craigowrie, capped by a boastful blue sky. But a parting of the grass, or rather a snaking line up the hill upon which the grass grew less well, drew me on. Was this the path upon which old feet trod a line from cart track to doorstep? Step by step, like a painting unfolding before me, I came in full view of the old house. The path got lost in a mire of withered brown rushes, the land unable to restrain these boisterous signs of sad neglect. But I knew the path nosed right up and bumped against the faded red door. The house still had a roof but the two black eye sockets which were windows only emphasised the decline, the emptiness. To me emptiness of this sort is uncomfortable, disruptive, noisy, even irritable. It's like knowing there has been a death; an unexplained death, an unnecessary death. You see, the emptiness is not just the cold, black hearth, the peeling floral wallpaper, the blue rusty enamel bucket, the soot upon the

33

crook. Emptiness is in the unkempt pasture, the blocked and overgrown drains, invasive rushes and thistles, the roofless steading of perfect grey granite walls bearing the date and initials of its robust builders; the dry well. And then there is the silent emptiness where you can hear the swish of long, black skirts hurrying round windy corners, the whispers behind doors which are lost in the lamentations of wind in the chimney. And there is the stillness – that of the stones themselves, so utterly deeply stilled. But far greater is the stillness of the hands which once ploughed and sowed, scythed and reaped; of the feet no more to walk the cart track or fall upon the doorstep. I turn my back to accept, if I can, what none of us could prevent – the death of a croft.

I bury the past and delight in the present but my powers of observation are dulled by melancholy and for a moment I'm conned into thinking I've discovered heather in bloom in June. Not the early bell heather or cross-leafed heath but ling heather. Pale pink and mauve flowers peep from brown twiggy heather shoots. I drop to my knees and discover milkwort. The same day I was to see three other colours of that delicate ground-creeping flower – white, royal blue and pale blue. Cheek by jowl with butterwort was the ungraciously named louse-wort, with a pretty fresh pink snapdragon flower. In Germany it is believed to give lice and liverworms to cattle. I didn't get that close just in case.

Little yellow buttons of radiant tormentil bloom, sprinkled over heath and grass wherever I walked. Containing dynamic qualities despite its size, tormentil is used to cure colic, diarrhoea and even cystitis. Below ground the plant's roots are said to help disorders above the belt, in particular the mouth, where if chewed it will harden the gums and keep the mouth clear of complaints. My reference book doesn't say whether mouth complaints mean halitosis or nagging!

I myself have been overtaken by fate for interfering with Nature. I tried to persuade two hens, whose genetic 'disorder' inclines them more to egg laying than 'clocking', to sit on clutches of hen and duck eggs. No matter how securely they were imprisoned on their eggs, in fact, anything less than barbed wire and metal bars, and they were off at the drop of a feather. They were fed and watered in their cells for the first three days, and when I let them out on the fourth day to stretch their legs, they ran half a mile, not for the exercise, but to avoid becoming a mother. The proud father to be, who had been scratching in the wings, looked up disconsolately as the cackling, screeching hens streaked past him. He looked quite defeated in his 'amazing uniform of a wildly foreign field marshal.'

Scented pathways of memory

Some people love the smell of newly baked bread; my grandmother loved the smell of bog myrtle. I thought of her last night as I walked across my common grazing, waist high in jade-leaved sweet gale, as bog myrtle is sometimes called. I rubbed the leaves between my palms and inhaled deeply of that spicy, aromatic scent, reminiscent of eucalyptus. A fresh pluck of leaves and I close my eyes, inhale more slowly, more deeply, searching down the scented passageways of my memory for her face, her voice, her laugh. My grandmother was descended from a Campbell family who had salt in their veins. Her father was a sea captain and lies buried in Port Stanley in the Falklands. When my husband was there last year he tried to locate the grave but failed as there were so many Campbells buried there and I had forgotten to give him the Christian name. My grandmother's brothers left boat building in Arisaig to build boats in Cairns in Australia where I believe there is still a boat yard bearing the sign, 'Duncan Campbell, Boat Builder'. But my grandmother stayed in Lochaber and took what fortune offered her which was a MacDonald of Clan Ranald.

I, too, love bog myrtle and believe its unique, dynamic aroma would not be out of place in the exotic spice markets of Indonesia or Zanzibar. My grandmother used bog myrtle as a sort of crofter's pot pourri, laying sprigs of it between blankets in her kist. I have a vague memory of her making little scented sachets of lavender, rose petals and bog myrtle to scent drawers and her linen cupboard. She was the most wonderful homemaker I have ever known, practising the art with skill and dignity. She could sew, smock, do intricate lace work, embroider, crochet, knit — everything from Fair Isle to cobweb lace shawls and a whole circus of knitted clowns. Her cooking and baking were only second to her Christmas dinner trifle which was as much a delight to look at as it was to eat. It sat in the centre of the holly and crackers, an awe-inspiring and mouthwatering arrangement topped with violet sugar pansies and blushing pink candied rose petals spangled with silver balls winking in the candlelight. I loved that trifle. But I also loved my grandmother and I'll never forget the contentment with which she lived her life. Nowadays, we all seem less happy with our lot.

Talking of candles and bog myrtle, you can make one from the other. There are tiny yellow glands along the sides of the twigs and leaves of bog myrtle which carry a wax which can be extracted by boiling the foliage in salted water. The wax floats to the surface, is skimmed off, remelted and strained. I think it would take a considerable quantity of the

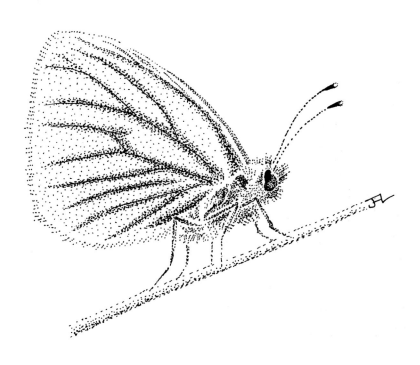

plant to make one candle. A sprig of bog myrtle, which has a sweet smell and a sprig of elder, which is acrid, tucked behind the ear is said to go some way to repelling midges. I think a discreet bottle of jungle juice in my pocket would better protect me and my reputation; after all, who ever saw a crofter with bog myrtle sticking out of his ears?

As I was putting ground to my tatties this morning the unmistakable bough! bough! of a roe buck rasped across the field from the forest edge. The dogs went hysterical as the chesty bark came nearer — they could see and smell no other dog but could hear barking. The buck eventually appeared and I recognised the bleached tips of his antlers and his dullish grey/brown coat. He clinked his antlers on the galvanised metal gate and nonchalantly scratched his ear with a Sheraton-like leg. He pushed under a pile of birch branches, sniffing — had some other buck than he stepped airily this way? He moved to the burn, dibbled and tippled for a moment before parading along the high grassy bank. He has such style, such panache — an accomplished performer. Who does he think is watching him — another roe buck, for sure. But he knows, and I know that in my hayfield lies a dinky, brand new fawn — his fawn. Eating only a leap or two away from this leggy, spotty bundle is the sunken-bellied doe, anxious, edgy, a rowan leaf caught in her startled mouth.

Rolling mists and reiving highlanders

'And what good is a bit of a farm on it, and sheep on the back hills, when you do be sitting looking out from a door the like of that door, and seeing nothing but the mists rolling down the bog, and the mists again and they rolling up the bog, and hearing nothing but the wind crying out in the bits of broken trees that were left from the great storm, and the streams roaring with the rain.' So wrote the Irish poet J.M.Synge in *In the Shadow of the Glen*. He describes most accurately my feelings of melancholy and observations of the countryside as we come to the end of another week of atrocious summer weather.

As I write it is a bad day by January standards with grey sheets of rain driving across the fields, the birch wood a restless green sea of a million wind-tossed leaves. The sheep stand backs to the north-westerly chewing a plentiful cud of clover and grass – the only consolation of this savage summer.

Strathspey with its now mythical annual rainfall of just over thirty inches a year was always considered a good drying place. Your peats would dry, your blankets would dry and your hay would dry. There was that high summer smell of warm resin in the pinewoods, with cones clicking and splitting open in the dry air, releasing their seeds. Now the pinewoods are dank and damp, the rain-sodden earth giving off a mouldy odour. But the rain keeps you fit, too, as you sprint from house to washing line, from peat shed to stove carrying a precariously loaded bucket from which one if not two peats will either tumble into a puddle or trip you up and pitch you onto the wet grass.

I had to sprint this morning to the big white stone sink in the old stack yard, which is half full of water and into which a baby duckling had taken a dive, enjoying the floating sensation, until his mum and siblings wandered off. He quickly discovered he was just not big enough to jump out and the slippery sides of the sink afforded no escape either. It was his panic peeping which first alerted me, a signal which the crows and jackdaws would also be receiving. But I can sprint faster than the crows can fly and I reunited the duckling with anxious mum. As a safety precaution I placed a large granite boulder in one corner of the glazed sink as a stepping stone for daft diving ducklings.

Looking out at the water boiling over the burn banks and my neighbour on the hill walking up my brae soaked to the skin, having misjudged the showers – not that he was skilled in any department that morning, especially putting one foot in front of the other after hectic nocturnal socialising – reminded me of some of the stories my grandfather, Allan MacDonell, used to tell his family of days long, long gone. He was an entertainer and bard of some distinction in Lochaber and always in great demand at ceilidhs with his pawky rhymes, in Gaelic of course, about local people. I was just ten when he died and don't remember very much about him but the old people of Brae Lochaber always tell me how he knew every hill and corrie, burn and tree in the district. But more importantly he knew the family and relationship of everybody in Lochaber. This sort of knowledge was of great value in avoiding interbreeding in what was considered an unlettered society. But back to my reference to rain-drenched land. My grandfather used to tell a story of how as a boy he sat at the feet of old men, storytellers like himself, who in their turn as boys, remembered listening to other old men, calling the clansmen, the Keppoch MacDonells, creeping back from Culloden at night, soaked to the skin, exhausted, hungry and wounded. This storytelling, the listening and repeating of history, of relationships and families is called 'Slionneadh' in Gaelic.

My father was not a storyteller, like his father, but he did have some memories, but at that time I wasn't very interested and was too busy bringing up a family. He's gone too and lies in the ancient graveyard in Brae Lochaber, Cille Choirill, along with his father, my grandfather. Not far away from them is the massive headstone of our other ancestor, the famous bard Iain Lom of Keppoch. They are all silent now with their gifted tongues and cherished culture. I wish I'd listened more.

Lochaber clansmen were renowned in the Highlands for their daring cattle-reiving exploits and at one point cattle stealing could almost be said to be commercialised. This dubious achievement could certainly be claimed by the Lochaber men who raided mostly into Badenoch but often ventured into the soft lands of Moray. However, they met their match in a most unusual way at the hands of somebody they'd certainly label an 'amadan' or fool. And he lived on a croft only a few miles from here at Dalnahaitnich, on the river Dulnain.

Little John MacAndrew was very small in stature but had tremendous courage and initiative and his skill with the bow and arrow was known throughout the Highlands. While returning from a foray to the lands of Rose of Kilravock, a strong body of Lochaber men passed through Strath-dearn on their way home with stolen cattle, when they were overtaken at Cro-clach, in Strathdearn, by Rose of Kilravock and MacIntosh of Kylachy, supported by numerous clan followers. Little John MacAndrew was also in Strathdearn that day and Kylachy pleaded with him to help them retrieve their cattle and dispose of the Lochaber men with his celebrated archery skills. John agreed and fought fiercely mortally wounding the chief of the raiding party with one of his arrows. When Kylachy saw this he imprudently shouted 'Tapadh leat fhein Iain Beag MacAindrea bho Dalnahaitnich, se do laimh rinn sud' — 'thanks to yourself Little John MacAndrew from Dalnahaitnich, it was your hand that did it'. Alert Little John was instantly aware of Kylachy's motives and replied angrily — 'Mile malachd ort air do theanga in Coillsach's eagal ort' — 'a thousand curses

41

on your tongue Kylachy and you afraid'. Of course, Kylachy's plan was to draw attention to John's part in the slaying knowing that the people of Lochaber would seek revenge and perhaps leave Strathdearn free of further depredations. Not a man was left alive in the raiding party, except a young boy who was acting as look out and witnessed the massacre of his clansmen from a distance. It was he who carried home the news of the tragedy.

When Little John MacAndrew returned to his croft he hid his bow and arrow in an old spreading pine tree ready for the revenge he knew was inevitable. The cattle raiders returned on a winter's day to kill Little John. His quick-witted wife, recognising the Lochaber accent, turned to her husband and ranted and raved at him as though he were an impudent herd boy sitting in his master's chair at the fireside. She drove him out of the house and welcomed the Lochaber men as belated travellers and apologised for her husband being away on the hill. She treated them to food and a dram while pretending to await her husband's return. Shortly she told the raiders that she could see her husband coming close, whereupon they left and one by one were slain by Little John and his bow and arrow. But he reprieved one saying – 'Go home and tell your tale'. A monument to the gallant archer stands at Dalnahaitnich and the mounds of the slain are still visible by the banks of the Dulnain.

Another version of this story refers to him as Ruairidh Troich or Roderick the Dwarf. He did not belong to Strathspey but was brought there by an eagle who snatched him from his parents as they worked in the fields. He was found near Dalnahaitnich by the tenants there and brought up as one of their own. He never grew to any size but what he lacked in stature he made up for in his many skills. He was a successful

farmer, holding large numbers of cattle and he married a local girl. He was such a skilful archer that it was said he could stick an arrow into the one that preceded it.

Eventually – a clipping

A rare and unexpected treat was thrust upon me last Saturday. I was forced to have a long lie. I say forced because I really don't enjoy lying in late; I'll get up even although it's only to sit and contemplate the view from my croft over my first stroupag of the day. However, last Saturday, after ten days of misty, mauchie, miserable weather, through which my three acres of cut hay became bleached and I became baleful, I decided that there was nothing better to do than lie in bed and wallow in self-pity at the plunging downward curve of my life.

The day had started badly and early at 5 a.m. when the collie began barking and whining to get out – nobody in the household made a move and as the impassioned pleas went on, roughly translated as – 'if somebody doesn't let me out there will be a dreadful mess to clear up in the morning'. I'm always the somebody who cleans up the mess anyway, so inverted laziness made me move. I opened the door to the most dreich morning I've opened my eyes to for a long time. The mist covered the Shepherd's Hill and the croft of the old caillaich just nestling on the treeline was truly blanketed in moist grey cloud. Not only that, it had been raining heavily in the night and my white sheets, water-logged once more, now reached the ground. The two cats shot past me glad of a warm, welcoming open door. The collie went a long way to do her business, Tomintoul I reckon, by the length of time it took her to come back – and that was after I had been standing for ten minutes barefoot on wet, cold concrete, whistling a very indifferent whistle. At 5 a.m. I'm rather dry of mouth and my whistle is not at its best. To cap it all the collie gave herself a most energetic shake right beside my bare legs. And that cold shower underlined the bleak fact that we wouldn't be clipping any sheep on Saturday. So you will well understand why I released the button on the alarm clock and hoped I would sleep until the sun shone again!

Nine o'clock came and I could hear Nan, our pet lamb, bawling for her bottle. I could hear the hens laying before their breakfast rather than after their feed as is usual. The dogs left me alone obviously sensing something pretty unusual was happening. But guilt was beginning to creep in and I started thinking what I could usefully do in the house as outside work was totally impossible; it was raining again. Perhaps we could paper the grubby ceiling in the kitchen. I soon discarded that idea as papering a ceiling is difficult and can lead to confrontation if not divorce and I still have twelve acres of hay to deal with as well as one hundred and twenty sheep to clip in the next two weeks. I felt domestic harmony was not to be tested with something as explosive as papering a ceiling!

As it turned out neighbours were at a loose end too and the morning was frittered away talking about the neighbours who weren't there. In the afternoon I continued the downward curve of my existence and watched television for three hours ending with a pie and chips in front of the box accompanied by a bottle of homemade wine. By ten o'clock I was completely exhausted and went to bed, the gloom from outside totally extinguishing my spirit.

The sun is shining. It is Sunday and my spirit, appropriately, has risen heavenwards towards that wide clear, blue canopy. I am ecstatic and give everyone who is still in bed, tea and toast. A working breakfast follows over which we discuss whether to clip the sheep or turn the hay. By the time the porridge is finished we've decided to clip. Dogs and men flex muscles and I bless the deep freeze in which sits the clipping dinner.

In the end it was the collie who couldn't last the pace, while the rest of us, lanolin to the elbows, sweatily clipped the last of the flock. Small, gentle Nell had done well answering the morning's bidding, racing like a fleeing arrow through the wooded low ground to the tall, tough heather on Meall a' Bhuachaille. Intent, dedicated and alert in both ear and eye she gathered sheep, her shoulders powering on like a chasing cheetah, carrying her across the hill. In the high green patches of Corrie Eagan, above Rynuie, three ewes and their lambs looked down on the quicksilver thread moving along the path towards the fank. Round an outcrop came Nell, her tongue flying over her shoulder like a pink scarf. The ewes hesitated for a moment, and Nell crept forward, the stubby heather grazing her belly. This unmistakable sign language understood, man, dog and sheep headed for the fank some two miles lower down.

Tea and scones revived the gatherers while the rest of the shearers sharpened their tools and the draggers rolled up their sleeves for their first introduction to cunning old ewes and surly rams. Having driven twenty beasts into a smaller pen we were about to start the clipping ceremony when the three Corrie Eagan ewes, identifying a loose strand of wire in the fence, made a bid for freedom. We were all mostly left wrong-footed with a ewe in one hand and shears in the other. By the time we roused Nell from her slumbers in the shade of the steading, the fleet-footed trio and progeny were well up the burnside. Try as she might, Nell just wasn't fast enough to head off the sheep as they raced away from her at an ever increasing angle. Despite even more pleading commands Nell was just too exhausted to deal with the escapees. As I shouted for re-enforcements, the clipping operation had to stop as six humans recaptured three ewes. Work underway once more, Nell joined us in the fank and slept soundly for the rest of the afternoon, undisturbed by the lamentations of the flock which ranged from girning lambs to quavering soprano protestations from neurotic ewes and to the throaty bass of rams.

The two apprentice draggers did well grabbing the black-face ewes by the horns for the three shearers. I was responsible for keeling or marking the beasts with 'paint' on the left shoulder which is our mark and for rolling up the fleeces which amounted to about one hundred and twenty by the end of the day. And I fussed over nicks in the skin, administering Stockholm tar to cover cuts and protect from flies. As it was my flock we were working on I provided the food and drink and the four bachelors in the squad much enjoyed the brandy-laced trifle before settling down to tea and iced cakes. While the 'crack' ranged from the skill and daring of hunting trips in years gone by to a new estate fence which is going to parcel us all up, I decided that as the tongues got looser the joints were probably getting stiffer and I gathered up 'the boys' for the final onslaught on the wary flock.

I took over the shears for a ewe or two while my neighbour on the hill had a smoke and recovered from clipping a boisterous hogg who had spring-loaded feet and had kicked him in tender painful places. He rose from the bucking beast, bloodied but unbowed and released it from his sweaty grip with a string of oaths barely heard above the indignant bawling of the beast itself. He rescued his bonnet which was now covered in red keel and told us in no uncertain terms that he was too old for all this carry-on – or words to that effect!

As we pull and drag, clip and sweat, roll and pack, a wall of thick, grey cloud comes rushing in from the west dissipating sunshine and cooling the still warm air. A drop of rain – or was it? Ten sheep to clip and everyone is working flat out. Another drop, and another. The last few fleeces were slightly damp so I lay them over the stalls in the byre to air off. With much gratitude and great relief I look at the several bags of black-face fleeces and one of cheviot and reflect on the current depressing state of the world wool market.

We had a small celebration at the clipping today – actually it was more that we celebrated the clipping with a small dram but in a historical receptacle. The container was a horn cup which held a very acceptable double whisky and has been in use at clippings and dippings in this township for nearly a hundred years. It had always been in the Grant family of Rymore and at a dipping between the wars the old bodach from Rymore, while passing round the drams, let the horn cup slip from his greasy hands into the dipper. It was retrieved after the dipper was emptied, and as you might expect, there's neither a chip or a scratch on the cup after a dipping and several thousand drams!

*   *   *   *

My pretty lapwings which delighted us all in the late spring have had their eggs plundered by hoodie crows. The same fate befell the three baby swallows in the barn. The parents were such a scatty pair of swallows that I never thought they would have the stamina to successfully rear chicks. I felt just as thrilled as they did with their hatch and just as angry and despairing when the crows snatched their babies. The pied wagtail's nest under the corrugated iron was similarly treated by the crows, the nest ripped asunder, the helpless chicks savaged by that evil black beak. This foul vermin is top of my hit list and will be destroyed.

Talking of objectionable youngsters, I think juvenile starlings must take first place. A pale brown squadron of about one hundred starlings landed one afternoon on the boggy ground around the well. They fought and squabbled, kicked and pecked, shouted and grumbled then flew en masse onto the telephone wire. They had obviously been told by accompanying adults to sit up there with their arms folded, or at least their wings folded and to shut up. You could see the mammoth effort taking place as they nudged and swayed and tried to push off the two dunces at the end who were facing the wrong way. This curious situation lasted about thirty seconds before erupting into another playground scene on the ground below.

Another task completed, but without much effort on my part, apart from signing a cheque, has been peat cutting. Along with the other graziers on the common grazing, I share the hire of the peat man from Tomintoul who trundles down Bridge of Brown with his peat-cutting tractor and comes to our side of the mountain to cut peats. A peat bank or peat moss traditionally goes with most crofts on estates hereabouts, a privilege I tenaciously hang on to. The machine lays the peats out in long lines and as soon as the three outer sides are dry they should be stacked to dry the under edge. So quickly have they dried this year that we've decided to take them home as they are – gratifying but grating on the hands throwing several thousand peats onto to a trailer. The coarse hands of summer are the warm hands of winter – translated into Gaelic that might easily pass for an ancient proverb and appear as a chapter heading!

Blessed sun — beautiful hay

If I were to be granted just one wish it would be to sleep for a week. That is how I feel after a week of hectic haymaking. Not only that but family and friends have arrived, escaping the oppressiveness of summer city life to head north to the sweet clean air of the Highlands and the charms of croft life. And the blessed sun has shone on haymakers and holiday makers alike.

What a gamble it all is this haymaking business. To cut or not to cut; to cut all or just half; to toss a coin or watch the weather forecast. I decided that as there was a new moon, just two days ago, we'd cut the rest of the hay and hope the new moon would bring warm settled weather. As the 'glass' or barometer rose steadily responding to the high pressure, I felt I'd made the right decision.

The seven acres with the heaviest crop were cut, leaving one three-acre field for later in case the weather broke and we were left trying to make all our hay in wet conditions. As it happened the hay made quickly and we were very conscientious about spreading and turning. As soon as the last sappy blade withered it was turned for the underside of the bout or swathe to dry. I was in charge of quality control and my decision each morning governed the order of the rest of the day. With haymaking you let everything else slide and go at it with a sort of desperate frenzy, always asking at the end of the day, for another fine day tomorrow and another one after that. I often feel it's a lot to ask, this perfect haymaking weather of blue skies, gentle winds and sunfilled hours — will there be a price to pay later in the season? It's all a bit like being ecstatically happy and thinking it can't last and that something awful is going to happen to destroy your wonderful state. I felt like that this week as I rose in the morning and looked for puddles on the tarmac. There were none and I was ecstatically happy.

To add to the complexity of our lives two of the cows were due to calf last week. One being a heifer meant a visit three times a day to their summer grazing on the lower pastures of Meall a' Bhuachaille. That was the first task of the day before stoking the Rayburn in preparation for the day's baking. It was always a race against time to achieve the first batch of scones before the men came in for their morning tea and before the sun spilt into the kitchen, raising the room temperature to an uncomfortable level. As I race up the track to the cows once more, having set various washing machines going, organised lunch and planned supper, I pass my neighbour's hayfields, a mechanical mish-mash of tractors and balers, turners and trailers, stampeding up and down dusty rows of pale green hay. As they clatter along giving birth every few yards to a small green bale, the whole scene has a sort of chuckling rhythm to it – or is it a frenzied momentum?

A stramash of cows round the heifer and I guess she's had her calf. It is a fine bull calf with an uneven white mark on its head, making it look slightly dopey. Nancy, the mum, already has her calf half dried and is settling down to being as placid a mother as her own mother, Polly, and grandmother before her. I am amazed how calm she is, allowing me to check over the calf, then continuing to lick and call to her sticky bundle. Soon she lets the calf suck without even lifting her leg to kick. Some heifers can deliver fairly hefty blows to their offspring, before they get used to the idea of a calf sucking their teats. I recall one day seeing Nancy's grandmother, Fraochie, my old Aberdeen Angus, allowing three calves to suck, without as much as a switch of the tail. Elated I race down in a cloud of stour to tell the haymakers.

They had started baling when I arrived and there was much expert advice flying around about the tension of the baler. But the advice fell on deaf ears for he who was controlling the operation was driving the tractor and couldn't hear, a bonus for me in the long run. The bales were a little loose, perhaps, but fine and light to carry for winter-time feeding.

I helped to gather the bales into sixes while the men stacked. By the end of the day we had worked over eight hundred bales. Exhausted we plodded from the fields, muscles almost refusing to function, hands burning from the nylon baler twine and wrists scratched with itchy red weals. The men collapse at the supper table, a look of exquisite pleasure on their faces as the cool refreshing beer rushes down their dusty throats. As I bend down to take a gigot of roast hill lamb from the oven my knees pled for mercy. If the weather holds, tomorrow will be another hayday, the only thing different will be the menu.

Had circumstances been different and the hay inferior, I had to hand an old alternative to poor hay. I found the 'recipe' in a tattered old book here at Inchdrein belonging to James MacPherson who first cleared the bog land to create this small green place. Entitled simply *The Farmer's Guide* it was written in 1834 by an Elgin vet called James Webb. He describes a visit he made to an 'active and intelligent' farmer, a Mr MacConachie from Keithmore (which I believe is near Dufftown) who had come up with a plan to compensate for the very poor and scarce hay that particular season. Apparently he had some old straw which was of use only for bedding his beasts and to help make up the deficiency in his hay he mixed the straw with some foggage or second crop grass after hay, which was salted and made into a stack. The vet's horse was stabled at Keithmore for the night and fed this composition which it ate as greedily as if it were the finest hay, leaving not a straw. So impressed was the vet that he managed to extract the method and ingredients from Mr MacConachie. A layer of straw and a layer of grass were alternately laid until a stack was finished, throwing some salt over every third layer. The quantity of salt was in proportion to the size of the stack but thirty-two pounds of salt was allowed for every one hundred stones of hay. The foggage grass had to be only half dried so as to allow for its sweating or heating in the stack, which meant that the juice of the clover or herbage impregnated the straw affording a very palatable bite for beasts.

*   *   *   *

Apart from a huge sigh of relief and a glow of satisfaction there is not much else in the way of celebration at the end of haymaking. I once stayed in central Sweden, near Storfors, on a farm where my family and I helped the farmer finish his hay, which was carted in loose and stored in the loft of the byre, which was an enormous wooden building. In this huge hay-neuk was a large trap door through which, in winter, the hay was pushed everyday to be distributed to the cattle and sheep below. By way of celebration, when haymaking was over, we were invited along with many other relatives of the farmer, to a special end of hay-making tea. This was taken outside and pride of place on the table was a many-tiered cream sponge out of which peeped delicate sweet wild strawberries, which the children had collected in the forest that morning. When we had each received a slice of strawberry cake, Carl-Erik the farmer, stood up and proposed a toast to celebrate a successful haymaking. Perhaps our own country dance, the Haymakers Jig, is the nearest we come to a celebration.

While on the subject of countryside tastes and earthy eating, I must tell you of another gastronomic experience while staying at Storfors. Carl-Erik was a skilled hunter as well as a farmer and during our time with him ate of land, river and forest. The most unusual, but quite the tastiest, was braised beaver which was much like white hare in texture and taste. There was usually pike or perch to start the meal, after which came smoked roe deer, beaver or roast elk followed by fresh cloud-berries and cream. Even the dogs were not forgotten, for instead of a marrow bone to chew on, the Storfors dogs gnawed on the flat spade-like beaver's tail!

The Wool Fair

A week ago saw the annual Wool Fair market in Inverness at which I got carried away and bought three cows and two calves instead of just two cows. Actually, that was the easy part; the hard part is the Monday morning telephone call to the bank manager. But the Wool Fair is quite an occasion in the Highlands though less so now than in days gone by. It is the last remaining fair of the important quarterly fairs held in Inverness. It was established in 1817 to sell sheep and wool and was attended by clan chiefs and country gentlemen, sheep farmers and 'mountain peasants', who assembled in Inglis Street to meet and transact business with south country buyers and wool merchants from Lancashire. It must have been an extraordinary sight with over a thousand people present and the Highland small farmers, which I suppose are our present day crofters, described as being 'clad in homespun tweed of various colours, the real aborigines of the country, tall, stout, athletic fellows, some in kilts, with their plaids thrown carelessly over their shoulder'. Whether it was because of the difficulty of transportation or a lack of suitable land and premises, no sheep or wool were ever present at the Wool Fair; the buyers knew the stock of each farm and made their deals without ever seeing either sheep or wool, exchanging only missives for delivery and payment. Over the years as the population dwindled and road and rail connections changed the marketing of stock, the Fairs died out and the Wool Fair became a horse market instead. Not all that long ago the horses for sale used to be paraded along the riverside by Bank Lane for viewing by prospective buyers. Nowadays in Inverness, with two auction marts, the fair is for both horses and cattle.

Last Friday well nigh a thousand people attended the Wool Fair between both selling rings. I was not carelessly clad in a homespun plaid and neither, sadly, was any one else there wearing the kilt. I fear we were a much less motley crew than used to do business in the relaxed manner of Inglis Street nearly two hundred years ago. In fact, nowadays, if you relax, take your eye off the auctioneer, you lose your bid and find that the beast has gone in the flick of the auctioneer's hammer. Auctioneers are an unusual breed of animal themselves, possibly a sub-species of the second hand car salesman. In the cosiness of group chatter before the sale he is your friend, you tell him what you want but up in his pulpit, above normal men and beasts, the laughing eyes turn cold and steely, the voice cracks like a whip, short and sharp piling on the tens, the hundreds. I wanted a particular beast and he knew it. I tried to stare at him with cold steely eyes too, to hold his icy glare so that he couldn't see the other bidders. I prayed for the last call to come sooner, for the clatter of his hammer. It comes – later; and she's mine. I'm hooked on this performance; twice more the ritual. The end result is pleasing for all concerned – the faraway farmer from

Wick who sold me his Simmental/Luing heifer due to calf at the end of August; and from the Great Glen I bought two Highland/Devonshire cows with calves at foot. All three beasts are red in colour, hairy of coat and sweet of nature.

I was thankful to get them home and I expect they enjoyed the feel of cool grass beneath their feet once more. Of course, there was a real stramash in the field as my black ladies met these three red intruders with their calves. After a career round the field led by my fifteen-year-old Aberdeen Angus of the bad feet, kicking her legs six foot in the air, there was an intensive sniffing session after which the new were accepted by the old.

Next morning all was quiet. Black and red beasts grazed peacefully on the creamy abundance of carpets of clover with yellow rattle and pink clover emerging in bright splashes here and there. A meadow of sweetness, beauty, light and scent. The tranquillity of the scene was enhanced by the rhythmical munching of grass, the gurgling burn, the distant bleat of sheep. No sound intrudes; no sight displeases. It's so uncannily perfect that I feel I will wake up at any minute and the illusion will be destroyed. But it is all so real, so normal and I am just so lucky to be part of it.

This heady trip on Nature's goodies restores me – I throw off yesterday's exhaustion and face tomorrow's overdraft with determined optimism.

AUGUST

The murder

Inside the foyer of police headquarters in Inverness there is a brass plaque which reads: *Erected in memory of Constable Thomas King, killed on duty, near Nethy Bridge, on 20th December, 1898.* The fact is that Constable King was murdered by Alan MacCallum who had been accused of poaching rabbits. Today rabbits are a plague, and no poacher would waste his powder on them. In the late nineteenth century poaching rabbits was considered a serious offence and as late as the second world war was a fineable act. In 1937 my neighbour was fined thirty shillings for shooting two rabbits. It's incredible to think that there were no rabbits in the north until about 1750 and that the clansmen who marched to Glenfinnan to join Bonnie Prince Charlie would have been familiar with the wolf but would have stopped in their tracks had they seen a rabbit!

In my view from the croft I can see the spot where Alan MacCallum shot Constable King. MacCallum had been fined for poaching in Abernethy deer forest on 6th December and had been in jail for similar offences. A local newspaper reported 'Not in the memory of the older inhabitants has there been a poacher so reckless and fearless'. Unscrupulous game dealers knew his name well; he was about to add murder to his crimes.

He had told a crofter neighbour who saw him on the afternoon of the crime that he had no intention of paying his latest fine for rabbit poaching. Speaking of his impending arrest he said, 'I'm going to take them as they come'. Constable King knew that MacCallum was not a man to come quietly – he was an imposing figure, tall, with a 'splendid physique', usually wearing home-spun tweed knickerbockers, hob-nailed boots and a double pleated Inverness cap. With this in mind King put thick padding in his tunic and remarked that approaching a desperate man warranted precautions. Both King and an accompanying officer, Constable MacNiven, were unarmed.

They entered the gloomy hovel, MacNiven searching the bedroom while King went to the kitchen. A shot rang out and MacNiven rushed through expecting to find a fight raging. He stumbled over something, struck a light – and found his colleague shot through the heart. His makeshift armour had proved useless. There was no sign of MacCallum. Three days later, deputy chief constable Hugh Chisholm along with two police officers from Inverness arrested Alan MacCallum in a barn about four miles from here and charged him with murder. On St. Valentine's Day 1899 MacCallum was sentenced to fifteen years penal servitude having pleaded insanity, a condition supposedly induced by the sun in South America where he'd worked for several years.

The family of the murdered policeman emigrated to Australia but MacCallum and the Kings crossed paths again. The exiles donated a prize for highland dancing to the Nethy Bridge Highland Games, and in a strange twist of fate, it was a descendant of MacCallum who was the first person to win the competition. A flowering currant bush alone marks the spot of the grisly result of poaching rabbits.

A town friend was visiting the other day and with the most laudable diplomacy asked why I had so many thistles around the place. He said he expected there was a good reason although he couldn't think of one. And he was right. There, bang on cue, as we stood looking at the most magnificent crop of thistles in the old midden, two velvet winged, perfectly patterned small tortoiseshell butterflies landed to suck thistle juice from the purple flower heads. The extravagant beauty of the scene answered his question and no more was said. Not only butterflies but a host of other insects enjoy the thistle nectar but late on when the plants are a mass of fly-away seed heads, the graceful goldfinch and the secretive siskin will feast on this prickly larder.

It was so late before I saw my first queen wasp, at one point earlier in the summer, that I thought the entire wasp population had perished. There are just a few around despite the hot summer and I asssume it must be due to a poor breeding season last year when July and August were very wet. Unlike hive bees, wasps, along with bumble bees, don't make honey and colonies are seasonal only, the sole survivors who live through the winter being fertilised females or queens. They hibernate, often in houses or barns, by hanging onto a curtain or rough surface by their jaws. And it is also with those jaws that the queen wasp excavates and builds her nest or bike by shaving off wood filings and making them into wood pulp paper with her own saliva. When this unique construction is complete, the queen wasp, having laid an egg in each cell, then has to forage for her brood bringing in countless caterpillars, spiders and other insects which she chews up and deals out from her own tongue to her hungry offspring. It is only after the first workers mature and take over the task of feeding the young that the queen can put her feet up or at least fold her wings.

I'm off to fold my own wings this balmy summer afternoon, metaphorically speaking anyway. I'm going to indulge in something I get a lot of pleasure from − picking fruit. In this instance it is hairy green gooseberries, the jelly from which will make a delectable accompaniment to mountain mutton and forest roe deer.

*   *   *   *

Home from the hill have come chirping flotillas of streaky brown young meadow pipits, perfectly smart in their first year plumage, as if just unwrapped from cellophane. Groups are feeding all around the croft in the long grass, building up their strength for their long migration over sand, sea and sierra to southern Europe, which as far as meadow pipits are concerned, is more hospitable in winter than Scotland. However, there are quite a few of these immature birds never destined to reach maturity, and I am ashamed to confess that our black cat has had a field day with these rather dopey birds. Not renowned as a ruthless, feline hunter, Tico was always more adept at getting the Brekkies out of the packet, than she ever was at killing rabbit and mouse in the wild precincts where other cats patrol and perform with distinction. Of course, once she had started, this newly emerged killer instinct ran riot and it was only after I'd found a larder containing three dead meadow pipits that something had to be done. So until pipit migration is over, Tico has special rations to subdue the hunting urge and induce daytime sleep.

Moon dance and Fair Isle

While living on the tiny Shetland island of Fair Isle in the 1960s it was interesting to note how greatly influenced the islanders were by the moon and tides. The waning moon was favourable for cultivation, reaping and cutting peats. Crops were planted if possible with a flowing tide and a growing moon and harvested with the tide on the ebb and the moon on the wane. Eggs laid with a waning moon were used for setting and this should be done at the first appearance of the new moon, since birds hatched during a waxing moon were difficult to rear. In some areas of Shetland it was believed that the cow only sought the bull in the first and third quarters of the moon and that if a cow was served in the first quarter a bull calf would result whereas if served in the third quarter a heifer was more likely. But the strangest story I heard while living in Shetland was that all pigs or 'grice' should be killed with a growing moon or else it would 'waste oot o da barrel'. The story tells of a young crofter who reared two pigs giving them identical treatment. Although his mother advised him to wait two days for a new moon, saying he wasn't superstitious, he killed one pig leaving the other for his mother who waited three days for the new moon before killing hers. The wisdom of his mother's advice was seen in the bacon, the son having to admit that his bacon simply wasted away to nothing in the frying pan.

I am holding the much maligned Tico responsible for the sudden death of a long-eared bat whose mutilated body was found, Mafia style, on my back doorstep. How the clever radar efficient bat didn't see the dopey black cat I don't know. All that I can think of is that Tico, third-rate hunter that she is, was not giving off any danger signals and the bat, confused by the supposed hunter's apparent indifference, swooped too close. Tico, with bat bait presented, snapped the moth-like morsel. Never a gourmet of adventurous food, Tico left the long-eared bat for me – to write about maybe.

Handsome black Polly gave birth to a sturdy bull calf last week. But was she served in the first quarter of the moon?

*   *   *   *

The Vikings called it Fridarey, the peaceful isle; the old Norse name was Fara, the far isle. Today, the name Fair Isle speaks for itself; home of the world famous knitwear, bustling white-washed crofts and a thriving community, Fair Isle is also a National Scenic Area and has the premier bird observatory in Europe. And it was to celebrate the completion of the redevelopment of the bird observatory that I was returning to Fair Isle for the first time in eighteen years. For eight years, from 1963 to 1971, my family and I had been warmly accepted members of that sea-washed, windswept community.

To reach Fair Isle my husband and I flew from Orkney in a tiny red and white Islander aircraft which was a bit like climbing into a tube of toothpaste, but exciting and rewarding as we flew at 800 feet above the sunlit north isles of Orkney. And everywhere the sea, a huge carpet of sparkling jewels disappearing beyond the white tumbling clouds on the horizon. It has been said that the Shetlander is a fisherman with a croft and the Orcadian a crofter with a boat. It was therefore hardly surprising to find the isles of Stronsay and Sanday, Westray and North Ronaldsay fertile and well-farmed with golden squares of ripening oats and barley and green fields grazed by cattle and sheep. From above we saw long strands of white shell sand alongside calm peaceful aquamarine waters. But close by this paradise the stone-walled cemetery with grey and white headstones is a testimony to some the sea asked back. Bountiful she may be to those maritime lands but occasionally, in a furore, she will keep some of those who take from her. Inevitable and acceptable to those living cheek by jowl with grey oceans.

But on we flew, the twinkling sea below, the blue sky above meeting perhaps in the long, grey distance where clouds over Norwegian mountains roll down to the sea. After the miles of empty sea a lump on the horizon is recognisable as Fair Isle and as it looms closer you realise with a sort of pioneering thrill just how isolated the isle really is. Twenty-five miles by sea from both Orkney and Shetland, it is Britain's most isolated inhabited island. Its cliffs are spectacular reminding one of a huge green jigsaw piece which has floated away from the Shetland archipelago, so well indented is the coastline.

The gravel airstrip, rebuilt from a wartime emergency strip, provided a remarkably smooth landing. I felt I'd never been away. Surrounded by smiling, friendly faces, warm hugs and handshakes and the unique Fair Isle dialect with, 'Whaur's du bin,' they asked, 'such a time you took to cam dis wey again'.

Rattling down from the airstrip the island looked a green and prosperous land with robust crops, sound, well-maintained houses and perhaps most noticeable of all, the high morale of the islanders. It is hard to believe that just over thirty years ago the spectre of evacuation raised its menacing head and Fair Isle was dubbed the second St. Kilda. This threat came about because the insurance agreement for the island boat, the 'Good Shepherd', stated that it should be drawn up on the slipway during the winter. There was a primitive hand-operated winch to do this job but it required a dozen strong men. When two families moved to Shetland and a third emigrated to New Zealand, there were barely enough men to perform this essential task and any further reduction would have meant the end of this lifeline link with Shetland, along with a human presence on the island dating back to the Stone Age. However, the then Zetland County Council came to the rescue and installed a power-driven winch. Since then the island has weathered many storms, both literally and figuratively, but with the guiding and bountiful hand of the National Trust for Scotland, the present owners, they remain a cohesive unit bound together by the common bond of love for this beautiful and historic island.

No more obvious was this than at the celebrations to open the re-developed bird observatory. After a sumptous meal the like of which one rarely sees on the mainland, far less on a tiny green dot on the high seas, there was a concert and dance. Most of the music was supplied by the musically talented Thompson family. They played and sang with melodic sweetness and light reminiscent of their own fair island. There was an emotional medley played on the Hardanger fiddle which sent shivers down your spine as the multiplicity of notes spilled out as clean and sparkling as the brilliant stars twinkling over the ocean outside. Young Ewen, a fiddle maker in the making, played perfectly a rousing set of Shetland tunes. His rosy cheeked grandfather told me that he was keeping a close eye on the 'banks' or beaches for, according to him, fiddles made from sea soaked driftwood made 'splendid instruments – the salt in da wood maks the music so sweet'.

As one lot of musicians retired another took their place, accordians, more fiddles and the spoons; the dancers took the floor. Boston two-steps, waltzs, reels and finally the Lancers, a dance of such complexity and high spirits that were the Vikings to land in the nearest geo, they would surely turn tail and run 'afore the wind from these skirling Fair Isle warriors. Such great good fun for all – bairns dancing with grannies, young bearded islanders dancing with incomprehensible visiting German maidens and husbands and wives hullabalooing with hilarity. Too soon it is midnight and Sunday, 'the morn'; we pick our way in the dark, arms linked, to the red Avenger with two white doors and a green wing, the Vauxhall tied together with assorted colours of baler twine. We drive the three miles from the north to the south end of the island with sleepy, sticky children on one knee and a fiddle case on the other. The wind generator goes off at eleven o'clock and it's to bed by candlelight.

Sunday and we have endless invitations to what amounts to two Sunday lunches, one supper and endless tea and cakes. By way of preparation, while the islanders were at church, we walked briskly to the north end finding an extraordinary citrine wagtail from Siberia on Golden Water and a very ordinary lesser whitethroat in cliffside bracken. Fair Isle, long famous for its rare migrants had come up trumps again.

The afternoon and evening of socialising were staggering and so special. We spoke of sheep and cows, of people present and those under a stone in the kirkyard; of seas and boats; wind and waves; of mountains and rivers, frost and blizzard.

Our last port of call on Monday morning was Lower Leogh and the retired skipper of the 'Good Shepherd' who had many times carried us safely through the grey, greedy seas of the Sumburgh roost. He has a new 'peerie boat' for himself now to fish for pleasure and because he has strong salt in his veins. We were still blessed by calm, kindly sea and I asked him if he was going fishing, to which he replied 'No. It's for no use on the sea this day, there's such a load of trash out to da wast the morn will be a venomous day'.

Tomorrow might be venomous but yesterday and the day before were magical filled with the warm, deep, enduring friendship of the Fair Isle people.

My sweet Alder — a tale of adoption

My sons described it as sod's law but I am much more philosophical about what happened to my fine looking cross Luing heifer while I was away last weekend on Fair Isle. I must confess that when I was faced with the catastrophe I did feel I had been dealt a pretty unlucky hand by fate. I had been away for just two nights, the first break in two years and I came home to a heifer who couldn't calve herself, had to have a Caesarean section after which the calf was found to be dead. I realise it would have happened whether I had been there or not and our splendid vet, George Rafferty, reassured me this was the case.

But checking the cow just hours before we left for Shetland she looked several days off calving but then she's one of my new cows bought at the Wool Fair in July, and as well as being a first calver, I am still getting to know her, unlike my own home bred cows whose moods and personalities I can read like an open book. While having my two day, two yearly holiday, my neighbour was attending the herd and noticed early on Sunday morning that the heifer was having problems calving. The hooves of the calf were just showing and it was the enormous size of them which worried him as he knew that the rest of the calf would be of similar proportions. The vet arrived expeditiously, the journey between field and steading being adventurous according to my neighbour's graphic description – a buckled metal gate proof of the heifer's strength and fear. The Caesarean section was performed with skill and the dead calf removed weighing some 246 lbs, which to my way of thinking, is a half grown calf. Alder, as I have called the cow, had been put in calf to a Simmental bull and I echo the vet's comments about it being 'inhumane' to put a first calver in calf to a Simmental bull. I personally always use an Aberdeen Angus or Shorthorn breed for beasts calving for the first time. If all goes well I then go on to use continental breeds and so far it has worked well.

With great difficulty I had to swallow, my bitter, bitter disappointment as I looked across, on my return, at my cattle. There was Alder, solitary, sad with a bulging pink udder and stitched belly. As I walked across she looked behind her and called gently for the calf that was never there. Salty tears ran down my cheeks in a mix of emotions from guilt to grief. There was a tiny spark of hope that I might be able to get another calf and try to persuade her to accept it — she was obviously still feeling slightly maternal but with heifers they soon forget they've had a calf and it's incredibly difficult to do this fostering. In my case this was exacerbated by the fact that Alder was wary of us and was also still anxious after her operation. I managed to locate a splendid week-old Freisian/Shorthorn bull calf from our local dairy farm at Tomdhu.

Next morning I started out with hope in my heart and ice in my veins on what was going to be a long, slow process at the end of which I could be left with a calf to be fed on the bucket and a cow needing her udder drained to protect her from mastitis. My versatile neighbour had performed the disturbing task of skinning the dead calf and I managed to secure this cloak of death on a very lively, bouncy wee calf. I called him Joe and wished him good luck as we put him into the large pen with Alder.

Both beasts ignored each other for six hours and it was now patently obvious that Alder had no idea that she'd given birth. The vet's advice to me to cut my losses and have the udder drained without trying, and probably failing with another calf, echoed inside my head as I stood eaten alive by midges with hope fading. Joe hated the smelly skin which was causing him to be tormented by flies. At one point the other cows moved into view some distance away at which point Alder saw them and it took me all my time to stop her from jumping the fence with her newly stitched wound. If she'd burst her stitches that really would have been sod's law. Seeing her agitation I thought I would take in two of the old reliable cows to keep her company and stop her jumping out in the middle of the night. She calmed down as soon as they arrived and for the first time walked over and sniffed Joe. For the next three hours she more or less did the same thing – but never licking, never calling, no real acknowledgement. Her udder was now alarmingly full. Dark, murky clouds rolled in from the west and a chilly grey mist settled on the Shepherd's Hill. The gloomy countryside matched my mood exactly. The two old cows looked at me with sad, sympathetic eyes as much as to say 'What more can we do – we're sorry'. It started to rain, heavy, saturating drops which the cows hate and they looked longingly at the shelter they know of in the wood. My neighbour arrived with his dog to check on progress. As we exchange greetings I thought I heard Alder give the ghost of a call to the calf – or was it my imagination cruelly playing tricks on me. My neighbour went into the pen, dog at heel, and we both distinctly heard a gentle, maternal lowing. 'She's very softly spoken,' says my neighbour. So there was a spark there after all in this sad, soggy scene.

It was now twelve hours since Joe had any milk and he was very hungry. We took the stinking skin off him and pushed both into a much smaller pen where Alder couldn't walk any distance from the calf. She had excellent long teats and Joe found them easily, to be swiftly kicked for doing so. We discovered she was much calmer if you spoke quietly to her and he discovered it was much safer to suck from between her back legs rather than from the side. He was a brave as well as a hungry little calf and he persevered. Surprisingly she never once butted him but just kicked. As his hollow belly filled up she became aware of what was happening and began to look quite placid. And then again memories of the last forty-eight hours perhaps came flooding back to her and a scared look came

70

into her eye and she became agitated once more. For the next hour this was the sequence of events until Joe lay down. I gave Alder a good feed of sweet hay which she munched at contentedly. The fostering trail had began fourteen hours ago and I was soaked to the skin but I knew that the calf would be alive in the morning and that Alder was at least half way to being a born again mother. As for the other two matrons – they had to be pacified with buckets of sugar beet pulp and promises.

At half past six next morning I lay in bed desperate to get up and race along the road to see how Alder and Joe had passed the night. I restrained myself for another hour and then, heart in mouth, stomach in a knot, we set off. A scene of complete calm and togetherness greeted us – Joe happily sucking a normal looking udder, his white tipped tail indicating his pleasure. Alder, peaceful, relaxed, mothering, anxious for Joe; the two old ladies totally cheesed off. I am overwhelmed; my spirits soar, the tears fall.

We took them back to the field to join the rest of the herd with much sniffing and nosey jostling from the other mums and offspring. Alder took Joe across the burn and hid her precious bundle in high bracken – she was taking no chances this time.

SEPTEMBER

Harvest ,

No period in the farming year catches the imagination as much as the harvest. Scottish literature abounds with references to it in prose, poetry and ballad and the entries in the Scottish National Dictionary under 'hairst' provide clear testimony to its place in the social and economic life of Scotland.

In the more rural areas, especially in the north and west, the harvest is sadly a thing of the past with virtually no barley or corn being grown. Where it is still grown on crofts the social side has diminished and the economic benefit is debatable. Having said all that we still grow about four acres of oats and will continue to do so for all sorts of reasons, most of which have nothing particularly to do with the social and economic life of Scotland!

Last Saturday was, rather optimistically, earmarked for the harvest – it suited everybody including the 'big' farmer from the banks of the Spey whose barley was a week off cutting. I had been praying the fragile September heat would hold and not be extinguished by rain and wind which would not only demolish the top heavy crop but would also mean a delay which in turn would mean we would have to accept the combine at somebody else's convenience. Preceding days were breathtakingly beautiful, nature combining all the elements of early autumn to provide a daily dose of spectacular scene changes. The temperature near to freezing most nights, the early mornings chilly and airish with solid banks of intensely cold grey mist down to tree level. At dawn a heavy, soaking dew clung to every growing thing, awaiting burn-off in the sun, which was almost red hot one minute, then cool, anaemic, mist-enshrouded the next. All this, I predicted, would mean an afternoon harvest but with only four acres to cut this was perfectly feasible and without worry.

It was a joy to hear the roar of the combine harvester as it trundled up the narrow road through the forest by Loch Garten. The negotiation of a variety of field gates with a twelve foot machine was executed skilfully with many times only an inch or two to spare. The driver stopped the combine to have a blether about the crop, lamb prices, collie dogs and other important topics only to find that his combine wouldn't start again. He'd been having trouble ever since it almost floated down the Spey in the February floods. He had only time to move his stock before the river marooned his combine. After a frantic search for battery jump leads everywhere from my knitting basket to the bathroom cabinet, after which we still had to borrow some, we eventually got the harvest underway. In less than two hours the field was cut and the corn in the grain shed, well over two tons of golden ripe grain spread across the floor like sun-kissed sand dunes in the desert. A surprisingly heavy crop considering the hens, ducks, rooks and finches had more than their fair share at sowing. It is reassuring to think that there lies a good winter's feed for the sheep and poultry with enough to bruise for the cattle besides. Baling the straw we'll leave for another week as there was a fair bit of grass in with it and that will need to wither, but again, oat straw will make very palatable winter bite for the cattle.

After a cup of tea, William and his combine were on their way but not before he'd said how much he had enjoyed cutting the oats. I looked at him quizzically to which he replied that he didn't often get the chance to combine corn, in fact, it was fifteen years since he's last cut corn. Of course, that is not surprising; with malting barley realising £150 per ton who would bother growing a puckle oats for sheep, hens, ducks and all the finches under the sun who have an open invitation to dine on my crop.

As I watched the giant yellow combine rumble off home I still had to pinch myself that the harvest was home and safe. It is only twenty-five years since the first combine was seen in the township of Tulloch yet the machine itself was first used in Scotland in 1932 by Lord Balfour at Whittingehame Mains in East Lothian. In very early times cutting corn was called shearing and done mostly by women with a huik or sickle which had a toothed cutting edge. In the late 1700s it was replaced by a bigger smooth-bladed type which was easier and quicker to operate. Oddly enough corn cutters in the south of Scotland stuck with this sickle until the coming of mechanised reapers, while in the north and north-east the scythe was introduced for cutting grain and in many parts of the western and northern isles was still in use in recent times. It was an Angus divinity student, Patrick Bell, who achieved one of the great agricultural advances of our time when he evolved the principle of mechanised scissors as a basis for a new type of cutting blade, of the kind that remains to the present day on reapers, binders and combine harvesters.

Inevitably, the social side of harvesting has totally disappeared with the advent of a machine which can cut and thresh in one process. Stooks and stacks have gone forever along with the threshing mill and the characters who travelled around the district for this community event. The last threshing mill at Inchdrein was in 1972 and we fortunately have photographs to remind us of the day and the people, many of whom have all their harvests behind them now. Every farm and croft grew oats, in earlier years for meal, and latterly for essential animal feed. Wildlife and birds in particular thrived on this abundance of grain but every now and again they got their come-uppance. My old aunt tells the story of how the capercaillie used to feed from the stacks of corn in the stackyard. She was an excellent shot and in the dark winter days when a crofter's diet was repetitive, a change of menu could be had with a game bird or two. One day there were twelve capers on the stacks, and having shot one, the others paused for a moment to watch it topple to the ground before resuming feeding. She shot another caper. The others watched it fall to the ground and started eating again. Once more this extraordinary behaviour was repeated and they only flew off when my aunt retrieved the dead capers from the bottom of the stack.

With the cropping year at an end with the harvest, I have much to be thankful for, not least of which has been the warm sunny summer which bordered on drought at times here on the croft but somehow or other the blessed rain came saving the grazing and greening, once more, the dessicated hillocks.

Death calls twice

Our lives this week have been touched by death; a gentle good-bye to an old member of our township and the bleak tragedy of a young friend. The abysmal, black grief one feels for a teenager, who had but a fleeting glimpse of life, is hard to bear. But the funeral of my neighbour's mother was, in many ways, a quiet celebration of her life, over fifty years of which were spent bringing up her family at the foot of the Shepherd's Hill. She knew pain and sorrow, peace and joy.

In her heyday, with her couthie Aberdeenshire accent and earthy way of thinking, the 'wifie' was a force to be reckoned with, whether it was haggling with the auctioneer at a furniture sale or sorting out the boys after their lengthy celebrations following lamb sales, clippings or a visit of the threshing mill. When necessary she could deliver hot tongue and cold shoulder with a turn of phrase which could cut a person's character to shreds with the precision of a surgeon's knife. Her wit too was immeasurably accurate and funny. I will always remember her comment about one of her boys who had risen in the morning with a throat like a salt mine and a head pounding with thundering hooves, drink having been taken to excess the day before. The 'wifie' was sitting by the hearth, 'gathering her brows like a gathering storm', when he came downstairs. Of course, he got an earful of insults about 'getting fou and unco happy'. With the combination of this torrent of abuse and the pounding, splitting headache, he decided life wasn't worth living, and taking the gun and a couple of cartridges, made a dramatic exit upstairs. After a couple of minutes there was the loud boom as the gun went off but no thud as might be expected. And that was that. The 'wifie' never moved from the hearth. Five minutes later her son appeared, and his mother turning to him said, 'So you missed again!' And the petticoat government, as he affectionately called his mother, ruled again.

I felt an immediate and tangible sadness as I went into the house after the 'wifie' had died. She lay grey and still in the ben room for neighbours and friends to pay their last respects. The hearth was black and cold; the room small and alien without her considerable presence. Her bachelor son produced tea and biscuits, a far cry from the hospitality his mother would have produced. There is no doubt in my mind and quite a few others, that she could make the best venison pies in the country beating Mrs Baxter, Mrs Beaton or whoever. It has to be said that she'd had a lot of practice at it, of course. A Hogmanay first foot dram was never served with the cissy, falderal petticoat tails shortbread, but with a muckle venison pie which not only helped to absorb the alcohol content of the evening but gave you the necessary strength to finish the round of first foot visits without offending anybody. At other times of the year she could put Joseph Walker to shame with her soaring Victoria sponge, black sticky gingerbread, 'spirited' fruit cake, melt in the mouth pancakes, all made with her own butter and eggs. It goes without saying that she was also an impressive hen-wife.

The 'wifie' was buried with a sense of loss but no grief, in the ancient graveyard at Kincardine Church, with its unique leper window, alongside other worthy women such as the Baroness of Kincardine.

It is strange to think that there is a loose connection between my neighbour's mother and the Baron's lady, both now lying in the shadow of gloomy Craigowrie. One of the cords at the funeral was taken by another neighbour by the name of Cameron, and it was as a result of the marriage of the Baron of Kincardine that the first Cameron came to Strathspey from Lochaber, of course.

The Barony of Kincardine belonged to the Stuart family, descendants of that notable hero, The Wolf of Badenoch. When the Baron decided to take a wife he sought to make a matrimonial union of some significance and chose the daughter of the powerful and great Cameron of Locheil. Despite his illustrious standing in the Highlands, Locheil was definitely short of a sovereign or two, and to make up for the bride's lack of dowry in hard cash, he presented the happy bridegroom with a dozen of the bravest and most handsome of his numerous clansmen. They settled well on this Strathspey estate, multiplied and spread forthwith. The story goes

that these hardy mountain types from the west never wore any sort of hat or head covering and were known as 'Sliochd na'n gillean maol dubh' – 'the race of the black bonnetless lads', for they were all dark haired. When the daughter of Locheil or the Baron's lady was dying she made a last request to be buried in 'her own native earth'. Despite this she was buried at Kincardine and her wishes were complied with in a very unusual way. Two paniers full of Lochaber soil were carried on horseback from the west to Kincardine and the Lady's last wishes were fulfilled as her native earth was deposited around her coffin.

Droving

The cows are now home at the croft from their summer grazings up on the cool windy hill. We walked them the three miles without incident and with much enjoyment. Perhaps it is something in my genes inherited from that notable, ancestral Lochaber cattle thief, Coll of the Cows, but I find driving cattle the very best of crack. Mind you, news of this animal movement reached them before I got there myself because when we arrived at the grazings, the herd led by Derraid was at the gate nearest home. We never use this particular gate at any other time, but herself knew by some means or other that it was time to go home. Perhaps it was the vibrations of the earth under her hooves, or the moon, or the length of night and day.

At one point the road drops about 300 feet in half a mile and so eager were they to get back that taking them down this hill was a bit like trying to hold the tide back. At the bottom there's a cattle grid after which the road runs through a neighbour's grazing in which he had about two hundred cows and calves. In order to avoid what at best would have been

a circus and at worst a bovine riot we had to turn our animal traffic smart left after the grid and divert them through a forestry plantation to join the road home later. I had already received inside information that a padlocked gate in the plantation could easily be lifted off its hinges which made life a lot easier for me and quite a few poachers too, I suspect. I had a grand news with my accompanying drover as the cows trekked through the forest roads enjoying once more the fibrous taste of heather. A rest and drink for the beasts before we joined the tarmac road and we, the drovers, had to forget our blethers and return to vehicle vigilance. Some people, and not always tourists, believe that cattle and sheep for that matter, can read road signs and use lay-bys like other road users and deserve abuse and horn blasting for not doing so. Many a time I have felt the heat of a car engine before the vehicle stops as I have walked in front of my beasts. Little do they know that Maggie of the short temper and long legs will put a sizeable dent in anyone's car at an unnecessary rev of an engine. Passing the township's still red and normal telephone kiosk, the cows take a track well-trodden by many a hooved animal before them and emerge directly opposite our field gate. Once inside, breathing deeply, sniffing delicately, dunging boisterously, they rest. The wee calves, exhausted by the unfamiliar trek, need sustenance. My little adopted warrior, Joe, sucks long and hard from gentle, sweet Alder who has now fully recovered, both mentally and physically, from her Caeserian section; blobs of milky foam fall to the ground. The other red cows, who are now part of the herd and have never been at Inchdrein, stand contentedly suckling. The scene is tranquil, rural to the nth degree; colourful too. Blue skies, bright green grass, gleaming black cattle interspersed with warm red beasts surrounded by birches in glowing autumn colours.

If we, and here I include man and beast, found droving exciting and interesting, then what followed was something of a milestone for us all. The next day we collected our bull, the first ever to be on the croft. Like most crofters and farmers who have to rely on artificial insemination or AI, I had begun to find it increasingly unreliable and difficult especially with the older cows. The Aberdeen and District Milk Marketing Board runs an excellent service and we've had many a good calf from their bulls. But the timing can be chancy and this year one cow came back four times to be served and still didn't produce a calf in the end, whereas a bull running with the herd cuts down the margin of failure dramatically. For several reasons, not least of which was to gain some good breeding stock, I wanted an Aberdeen Angus bull. And that is where my plans went adrift because black bulls are few and far between in Strathspey, that land of quality stock and stocksmen. I was invited to join the Dorback group of crofters who hire their bulls from the Department of Agriculture but at present are working with Simmental bulls. I turned to Jim MacConachie of the Strathspey Farmers' club who said, 'It'll nae be easy, but I'll see whit I can dae for you, lassie'. He did plenty and a phone call the next night instructed me to collect a three year bull from Gaich near Grantown on Spey. It didn't belong there either but was on loan from Congash, near Cromdale and having served the heifers at Gaich was 'booring' to move on. Collecting him was fortunately free from incident although as he charged down the hill towards the open float I realised with sudden clarity the meaning of the word bulldoze. However, as he reached the ramp his massive bulk stopped abruptly and he walked demurely into the wagon. Obviously he enjoys the travelling life spending a few months at different farms with dewy eyed heifers. The aluminium float shook to its rivets as he turned round for a fond farewell to Gaich. 'The poor loon,' said the young lad helping, with obvious affection.

A slow journey home and the bull released, trotted heavily towards my herd. There wasn't an uproarious welcome but one or two of the young members came forward interested. But the old cow looked at me and I swear she shook her head as much as to say – traitor – for it is a matriarchial society here at Inchdrein and we don't suffer males gladly!

But we will be tolerant and kind to the bull for he has already earned his keep. What I will never forget is the kindness of the Strathspey farmers who rallied round and found me a fine black bull and trusted me with him for three months. A breed, in themselves, without equal.

*   *   *   *

A pre-lunch walk in the forest of Abernethy was made all the more enjoyable when a flock of twittering long-tailed tits flew over as I admired the stone work of an old limekiln. They chattered amongst themselves as they bobbed and dipped through the young fir trees, which were hanging with sparkling jewels as the sun caught the suspended rain drops on their branches. It may sound twee to say this but long-tailed tits are such fun – their rosy pink, grey and black plumage, elegant long tail, ridiculous tiny bill, make them one of our cutest woodland birds. And they have a delightful high-pitched contact call. Throughout winter they use this call to keep together as they are only able to survive the cold winter nights by roosting in close body contact with each other. Their survival depends on the group and so their contact calls are a real matter of life and death.

Half way up Cairn Rynettin we came across a tree which stuck out like a sore thumb among the birch, juniper and Scots pine. It was a whitebeam quite out of place in the heights of Strathspey but growing boisterously nevertheless. Our attention was first attracted by the large red rowan-like berries and the back of the leaf which is a fluffy white. The white leaf is characteristic of this tree for when the buds open in the spring the young leaves are coated with a thick woolly down giving the appearance almost of white, floury leaves. The blossom of the whitebeam resembles rowan flowers but the berries are oval and larger although when first formed are also covered in white down which gradually wears off to reveal rich red berries which birds as well as hedgehogs and squirrels love. Traditionally in France people planted whitebeam to protect their vines of all things. Apparently a great number of insects damage the young vines in spring but are eaten by small birds. However, when winter comes and there are no insects the birds can feed on the whitebeam berries and be around the next year to protect the vines once more. I daresay, nowadays, that vineyard owners turn to chemical sprays instead of whitebeams and birds.

OCTOBER

Shepherds, auctioneers and poachers

It's been a week of gathering, dipping, batching and keeling. In other words we have been getting our lambs ready for market. Gathering and dipping came first and we went along to help our neighbour with his flock. So many of us turned up to help that it was a fairly leisurely affair at which the men did all the hard work and myself and the old bodach from the next hill farm, leant on the gate keeping the others right and making wise comments. The strength of the shepherds is remarkable especially when faced with a thrawn black-face ewe or surly ram who knows what it is all about. A break in the proceedings allowed the sheep to drip dry and the dippers to mop their brows. It is always at such times that the older bachelors in the squad come in for barracking about not having a wife or housekeeper. Most of them have an old cailleach at home by the fire and probably find coping with a vitriolic old mother is enough without getting hot tongue from a younger woman as well. Having laid the old chestnut to rest until next year's clipping the hullabaloo starts again –

> and dogs hysterical with smells,
> sit on high haunches – sudden
> brawls explode and settle around a stick.

Our own flock's baptism came next and I was required this time to submerge the beasts in the tank for the legally required time after which they emerged skinnily dipped. An old cunning Cheviot performer, tight of coat, escaped my husbands's grip, took a flying leap to land with sheets of dippy water spraying everywhere, in my eyes, mouth, down my neck.

Despite smelling like a public loo which has just been washed down in Jeyes fluid I was happy to have the dipping past.

Batching for market came and went today with only one colourful incident. So that I would be well organised on market day I decided to colour code my ewe and wether lambs in order to recognise them instantly as they came off the lorry at the mart and separate them quickly without turning them upside down and peering up their backsides. I was standing in the pen with a tin of red keel marker waiting on the beasts to calm down and stop hurtling past me when they suddenly changed tack and almost piled on top of me knocking the tin of keel out off my hand and leaving two thick dollops on two lambs who immediately pushed back into the pack leaving a red 'smeurachd' on each one. Needless to say I too, received my fair share of this indelible marker. So if you are at the lamb sale in Grantown on Spey and you see a red faced, red necked woman selling red coated lambs no comments about scarlet women.

*   *   *   *

Despite dismal weather and droukit beasts the lamb sale in Grantown was a jovial and well-attended event. Although the prices were also slightly dampened, most farmers looked cheerful, their rosy cheeks glowing with the effort of separating ewe and wether lambs and working out the complexity of the gate system at the Grantown mart. Open the wrong gate and a hundred broken-mouthed old ewes, who know their appointed hour has arrived, will take off with amazing alacrity for the nearest open ground. The Grantown mart, though, is a cosy, friendly place mainly because you have to huddle together to avoid the rain coming through the roof of the rusty Nissen hut. There are one or two other facilities lacking — a weigh bridge for cattle, for example. I am selling a stirk this week and would be interested in his weight. When I asked the auctioneer about this he told me there would actually be one there on Thursday for a special occasion. As my eyes lit up he quickly extinguished the spark by telling me cruelly I was ineligible as it was only for young farmers! There is nothing worse, in the company of other farmers, than an auctioneer with a loose tongue!

Talking of sheep and animal movements, there are eight holdings in the view from the croft which were cleared in 1869 to set up the Abernethy deer forest. They moved to the bog land of Tulloch from the fertile green pastures at the foot of Meall a'Bhuachaille. It must have been a bitter pill to swallow for the proud Smiths of Rynuie who not only had their whisky stills strategically placed about their croft but also because they were renowned and skilled poachers. As a result of the scarcity of deer in Abernethy, the Smiths travelled across the Cairngorms to Mar to hunt their deer. Most famous perhaps is William Smith who was not only a defiant poacher but a passionate poet. His epic work *Allt an Lochan Uaine* is a delight to those who know what it is to hunt in misty corries and lie in a bog on your belly until the keeper's 'scope is back in his pocket again.

There are many fine stories told about the good old days of poaching — that's a personal opinion not an approval. Both stories I'll tell you concern the Smiths of Rynuie. William Smith had for years a long running feud with a John Munro, the stalker from the Braemar estate of Mar. On one occasion Smith had climbed a rock to spy for deer and was spotted by Munro who took up a position at the foot of the rock, sending another stalker to tell his wife he had trapped Smith and would not leave to eat or drink until he had him in custody. Two days later Munro arrived home very upset and obviously without Smith. 'Well, he saw you anyway,' said the stalker's wife pointing to a piece of paper pinned to his coat on which was written;

> 'Here lies John Munro quietly at rest,
> If he never wakes again, quietness is best.'

Because most of Smith's hunting was done on the Braemar side of Cairngorm it was necessary for him to have some sort of shelter to deal with the carcase and run to in bad weather. Smith and his brothers were masters at getting a beast off the hill in record time. In their crude bothy on Derry Cairngorm they skinned and boned the deer because it was worthless and exhausting to carry bones back to Rynuie. They also ate those parts which could be consumed immediately without hanging — heart, liver and kidneys. This allowed them to carry little food with them on a hunting trip but nevertheless to be well-sustained. On another occasion the keeper from Mar caught up with the deer bandits of Abernethy at Loch Etchachan. It was a crystal clear night, sparkling stars in the heavens, intense, crunching frost on earth. Caught, quite literally red-handed, the Smiths and the keeper shouted at each other, the abuse echoing around the empty loneliness of this high, frozen loch. The brave keeper ordered them to surrender both booty and firearms at which suggestion the Smiths grabbed him, smashed a hole in the ice and pushed the keeper under the freezing waters. They kept him there until he promised never again to halt or hinder their forays into Mar. The story goes that the keeper staggered home but died a week later of pneumonia. Personally I think the keeper's death is just folklore fabrication to create a goodies and baddies' happy ending. Here in the township there are a few poaching characters roaming in the dark green woods and heathery high hills but, like William Smith, their stories will be better told when they're gone.

Graves – dogs and witches

Fortunately I am not frightened in the dark; unfortunately my dogs are. Sometimes it happens that I don't have time to take them for a walk during daylight hours but if it's a reasonable evening without thick cloud cover, then we'll go on a well worn, well known path for some fresh air and exercise. Walking recently in bright moonlight, through some thin birches we came upon the dogs' graveyard. Dogs down the years have been buried in this sandy hollow, and at a rough guess there could be about twenty in this canine cemetery. They are not all dogs from the croft but a few people from the village have asked to have their pets buried here. Perhaps not quite the dog's last dying wish but it certainly helps the owner to come to terms with losing their dog if they know he or she is lying in what would have been a happy 'walkies' sort of place. In fact, my teenage son used to earn pocket money as the dog gravedigger, performing the necessary interment and comforting the owners.

I remember well some of the characters who are there – mostly clever collies who were sometimes better at performing tricks than their trade. My aunt had an old collie called Fanny who was a gentle, intelligent loyal dog. In the evening, after a hard day's work in the fields, my aunt would sit down to take her boots off. The faithful Fanny would not only untie the laces but would completely unlace the whole boot. And then there was old black and tan Ned, who was my great uncle's dog and a toothless horror he was too – the dog, not my uncle, although in his dotage my great uncle was that too! Anyway, old Ned lay under the table where he had lain all his working life. At meal times if you as much as flexed a muscle in your leg he'd snap at you with his stumpy black teeth and hard pink gums. There was also psychopathic Spot, whose brain never seemed to have cooled since having distemper and who always sat with his ears bolt upright, his eyes rolling like fiery whirlpools.

However, to get back to my two 'ablaich' – as soon as we came in sight of the graveyard the two dogs stopped in their tracks, very alert, not moving a muscle. The atmosphere seemed quite friendly to me but obviously not to them. Had they heard the snap of old Ned's jaws, a frustrated whine from Fanny as she tackled a knotted lace or had they seen the mad glitter of Spot's eyes? We all stood, holding our breath, for a long moment – the air was thin and clear so that even a sigh would have been clearly heard. Nothing moved, especially the shadowy mounds of the graves, I was glad to see. I said in a loud whisper to the dogs 'What's wrong, girls?', at which they leapt back behind my legs as if I'd roared 'here comes the Hound of the Baskervilles'! The place still seemed normal to me, when right on cue a tawny owl hooted, just above our heads. I must say that added a touch of theatre to the whole scene, and as I was without my so-called guard dogs who were quivering at my heel, I thought I ought to move on. For the rest of the walk the dogs wouldn't relax and run ahead as usual – they trotted behind me as much as to say 'No, you go first'!

Talking of 'bogles and ghosties, and long-legged beasties', albeit in their graves, gives me a fine opportunity to tell you about our famous grave in this township. It isn't in an ordinary graveyard or even a dogs' cemetery for it is the grave of a witch. The gravestone lies flat on the ground and on it is clearly and carefully carved the word WITCH. Also on the stone is the trade mark of the mason who carved the stonework. Nobody knows the name of the witch but we do know she was shot by Peter Smith of Rynuie, a member of that powerful family of poachers and whisky makers. I believe the killing of the witch took place in the early 1700s. Peter Smith was coming back from market on his horse and cart with a boll of oatmeal – about ten stone in weight – when the witch leapt from the bank of a burn threatening to cast a spell on him if he didn't hand over his oatmeal. It was well known that you could gain favour with witches and fairies if you left milk and meal out for them. Peter Smith refused to part with his meal and there ensued a very fierce argument with angry curses flying through the air with great vehemence. To put an end to this evil torrent, Smith took up his gun which would have been standard equipment on any journey in those days, and shot the the witch. Whether she was burnt before being buried, I don't know. Nor do I know whether Peter Smith became a local hero but what is known locally is that he willed the gun with which he shot the witch to his nephew, who rather than accept such a 'notable' gun, emigrated to Canada, never to return to Strathspey for forty years.

I was away with the fairies last week myself and have only just come down to earth. My beautiful black stot, Fergus, achieved the top price of £580 at the calf sale in Grantown last week. He looked splendid in the ring. Soft and placid by nature, but totally brainless, he had a magnificent body and should have been called Adonis. His new owner from Perthshire spoke to me after the sale to ask for his parentage. He is a noted Aberdeen Angus breeder and was so impressed by Fergus that he intends to show him. To me that was more rewarding than all those shekels!

NOVEMBER

The Gate Wife

There is nothing quite so uncanny as stepping outside in the morning and hearing a sound which should not be there. You stop in your tracks, shake the confusion out of your brain and decide, yes, it is November and not May, and why is there a curlew singing? And why is the song of the curlew, a wading bird of moor and marsh, coming from the top of a birch tree? They should all be plowtering around in the pollution in Longman Bay at Inverness. Another haunting burst of curlew trilling erupts from the leafless branches. He's managed to trick me again; this Mike Yarwood of the bird world, a lusty starling, his spotted coat iridescent in the sharp morning light, proclaims that anything a curlew can do, he can do better. And he mimics the curlew with uncanny accuracy – not just one verse of its song, but several, tone and pitch perfect.

There is nothing more accommodating than a cow who will calve at your convenience. Fraochie, mother of the fellow who went down the brae not so long ago for the big price, was a week overdue. Yet she was still on the go last Thursday morning, pushing and shoving the bull, twice her size and strength, for the sweetest blade of hay. A greedy cow by nature, she is affectionately or disaffectionately, as the case may be, known as the 'Gate Wife' because of her ability to push open gates. She once did just that and gorged herself on half a hundred weight of layers' pellets which almost killed her. However, she just as readily downed the gallon of milk of magnesia from the vet, which subsequently saved her life.

When I came home in the late afternoon there was no sign of herself and I eventually found her under some trees doing nothing in particular but just letting me know that she'd be calving shortly if that was convenient. Well, yes, I thought that suits me, but as it was getting dark, if I opened the gate, might she consider going into the warm, dry, lighted byre – just in case. Only at a price, I discovered – well, a bucket of turnips was fair exchange for peace of mind. So after the turnips, two flakes of hay and a bucket of water and, with nothing better to do, Fraochie gave birth, efficiently and without fuss. By the time I'd fed and watered myself she'd dried a fine black bull calf, who was unsteadily trying to suck. All the time she licked she called to him in a tender, loving, maternal rumble. I often think it is odd that we human beings don't communicate more with our babies at birth as well as throughout their childhood.

An intriguing factor came to light the other day while helping my neighbour with his birch. There was a pile of birch on one side which I started to throw into the barrow. 'Forget that,' he told me, 'it won't burn, it is as dour as a wet peat.' Apparently this particular tree had been struck by lightning, the brown scorch split clearly visible on the bark. He remembered his father telling him that any tree affected by a lightning strike wouldn't burn. Coming across just such a tree he decided to try it, but his father was right. I wonder if this elemental force somehow changes the texture or the sap in the tree rendering it 'dour' to burn.

Why is it that things nowadays are never like they used to be? My neighbour of the burning birch used to regularly see salmon up to spawn in his burn at the foot of the Shepherd's Hill. Nowadays you will hardly see one or two a mile downstream. But in those distant days when things were as they used to be, the greatest sport used to be had in deep pools with torch and gaff. I well remember one night of my misspent youth lying on a damp bank, under the moon, gaffing salmon. It was so easy

and so illegal! When we came home we emptied two sackfuls of fish onto the kitchen floor of the old crofthouse, their slimy bodies slithering all over the green linoleum floor. It was admittedly a small room but the whole floor was covered in salmon, their silvery backs glittering in the gentle light from the Tilley lamp. Today it would look like something out of *Whisky Galore* but then it was an annual event. With no deep freezers because we had no electricity the fish were distributed around the township with the kelts being boiled for the hens.

Russian cure for a crofter

The triumphs and tears in Berlin this last week or so reminded me of a story of east/west communication, some sixty years ago, involving a Fair Isle crofter. The old man associated with the tale, George Stout of Field, told it to my husband and me when we lived on the tiny Shetland island in the 1960s. Affectionately known as Fieldy, George Stout was a gifted observer of rare birds and could identify many obscure species from Siberia and lands east of the Urals, without the help of binoculars. Because of this skill he corresponded with learned ornithologists in countries behind the Iron Curtain comparing notes, or if a particular bird stumped him, he'd shoot it and send the skin to colleagues, perhaps in far-flung Moldavia, to be identified.

When he was getting on a bit in years Fieldy developed pernicious anaemia, and in a letter to a professor in Georgia, in southern Russia, complained about the weekly injection he had to endure to keep well. Back came a letter from this Russian academic suggesting a form of treatment used by the peasants in Georgia, where the incidence of pernicious anaemia was apparently higher than average. It also appeared to be less painful than the weekly jag.

Despite their blood disorder these mountain people of Georgia also lived to a ripe old age, many attaining 100 years. The secret was to live and breathe in a constant atmosphere of animals' breath. This was easy for the Georgians to achieve as their animals were housed below the first floor flat in which they themselves lived. A few well-placed holes in the ceiling must have somehow provided an adequate dose of vitamin B12, the factor at fault with sufferers of pernicious anaemia. Of course that system of animal husbandry just didn't apply in Shetland and Fieldy racked his brains as to how he could constantly live in animal breath. The answer was staring him in the face as he sat by the fireside, his sheepdog at his feet.

He managed to acquire five more collies and kept the six dogs in his croft house, religiously inhaling deeply of their exhalations. Unfortunately the clinical trial with canine vapours ended abruptly one day when Fieldy was out beachcombing after a south easterly gale. When he came home the door of his croft was wide open and all that remained of a pair of lambs on a tether in front of his house was the rope. An undistinguished end to some east/west frontier cooperation and a gloomy return, for Fieldy, to the termagant district nurse and her hooked needle.

Bird table menus

Some Spanish friends staying last week, were amused and more than slightly mystified when after feeding all domestic animals, I went on to feed the birds. Topping up the bag of peanuts to hang in the garden was a totally new experience for them. In Spain people would never dream of feeding birds, basically just to look at them while you eat your breakfast. They find it difficult to understand our obsession with bird tables and hanging feeders of every conceivable shape. I'm a bit stingy at feeding the birds actually and will only feed in severe weather. It seems pointless to me to feed them peanuts when there is a perfectly adequate supply of natural food on my own doorstep. There must be millions of tons of peanuts imported to Britain just to feed our birds – from Argentina apparently. I do hope they are not cutting down the forest to grow peanuts so that we in Britain can feed the bluetits.

However conscientious you may be with your peanuts and suet, birds can turn up their noses without ruffling a feather and eat the most awful swill. Several years ago my old aunt used to empty her teapot under a lilac tree in the garden. Over the years quite a considerable pile of teabags accumulated. During a spell of quite ordinary winter weather, with neither hard frost or deep snow, four bulky, heavy billed parrot crossbills descended on the teabag tower, and tearing the perforations asunder with more skill than one could achieve with a pair of scissors, proceeded to down the tea leaves. They worked away at the teabags until the pile had disappeared and we couldn't drink enough tea to keep up a steady supply. I have saved soggy teabags since but with no crossbill spectacle. These parrot crossbills from Scandinavia are a bigger and bulkier bird than our own Scottish crossbill and occur in this country when there has been a population explosion in the breeding forests as a result of a very successful season.

The other bully bird around at the moment is our local mistle thrush who has a desperate time trying to protect his winter supply of berries from the marauding Scandinavian thrushes. He goes bombing around the

rowan trees attempting to flush the intruders from the berry abundance. The mistle thrush makes a strange sound when doing this — it's a sort of sinister s-s-seep which occasionally works and the fieldfares will spill out of the tree in an untidy tumble.

Still on the subject of feeding birds but a million miles from the peanut syndrome — a Forestry Commission friend was telling me that while out stalking in Morven, near Ardnamurchan, twenty-eight ravens were circling overhead waiting on the gralloch. They have worked out that a rifle shot means a good feed and appear on cue each time, patrolling sky and cliff for their grisly bird table gralloch.

*　　　　*　　　　*　　　　*

In Shetland they say —

> 'If he's frost in November tae hadd up a duck,
> Da rest o' da winter is slush and muck.'

Well, I'm all for a mild open winter, despite the gutters. The recent frost was piercing and intense and seemed to be upon us before we knew it had happened. The ground was ringing like iron and my old cross Jersey cow, heavy in calf, was more than a little anxious walking up the frozen rutted hill on her spindly elegant black legs. Some folk locally still haven't got their water supply back after the sudden grip of the frost.

It was as a result of frozen water that I now find whisky so unpalatable. About twenty-five years ago, before electricity and piped water were known in this township, we went first footing one Hogmanay to a bachelor, who was not unfamiliar with strong drink. Being fairly young at the time I thought I was being quite adventurous asking for a sherry. After a scurrilous tirade on that particular beverage he said I had to have a whisky. I was slightly nervous of this huge red-haired farmer, who was more than a little tipsy, so I agreed to the whisky but with plenty of water. 'Go you to the closet, there's well water in the enamel pail,' ordered my host. So there was, frozen solid, even inside the house. I managed to down two teaspoons of whisky in half an hour and have never forgotten the experience.

As I write I can hear the exuberant green woodpecker yafling away in the bare winter birches, his wheezy laugh striking an odd note in the somnolence of a heavy, grey November afternoon. But all of a sudden a roaring yellow monster explodes amid the drifting mists and drowns out all sound; it's Monday and it's Badenoch and Strathspey District Council's dust cart!

DECEMBER

Proof against winter

It was Richard Adams writing in Watership Down who said, 'Many human beings say that they enjoy the winter, but what they really enjoy is feeling the proof against it'. And I am no exception.

Winter arrived last week, if we take snow and sleet, frost and ice as indicators. Just when winter sports businesses in Strathspey were beginning to get twitchy with the approach of the skiing season, the snow arrived. The mountains, as opposed to my hills, are now a true blue intense white, compared to the dirty white of the week before. However, one old hand on the skiing scene told me he didn't really want snow first but some hard, piercing frosts to refrigerate the mountains so that when the snow fell it would lie deep and crisp and even.

I do feel a certain peace of mind as I look out on the white-capped Shepherd's Hill, silhouetted against slate grey clouds, while a stuttering fire casts dancing shadows in the darkening room. All year from spring sowing to summer growing to autumn harvesting, has been an unremitting task to provide that proof against winter. For three seasons we toil in everlasting hope, to assuage the avarice of that fourth season. We know not of the vigour and mastery of the coming winter and whether our preparations with soil and sun will keep pace with its supreme authority.

The dutch barn is full of well made hay, sweet and light. Even feeding well into next April, I will still have a safety net of over two hundred bales left over. The grain shed holds more proof; four tons of hard, dry corn to be fed direct to the ewes or bruised for the cattle, and of course, an everyday breakfast for the poultry. There is the oat straw, too, for this and that, bedding in the old byres if we're pushed by weather and have to take the cows in; or for an extra feed when grittily laden sleet showers chill to the bone.

Yesterday, we cropped the best and biggest of the turnips and they are snuggly protected in a lazy man's pit of straw bales in the barn, along with a couple of hundred weight of precious Golden Wonders. The cows and sheep are now strip feeding on what remains of the turnip crop saving the more versatile hay for whatever is to come.

Two sheds were bundled full of peats in August, dry and hard and as fragrant and warm in the burning as the summer was in the cutting and gathering. A huge tumble of silver birch logs reaching the roof of the stick shed will last a month but that is a resource we'll be able to replenish throughout the winter. But stacked away carefully, in fact, almost cossetted, are twenty blocks of 'rossit', dry and sticky, to quickly light and cheer.

The minister's Christmas visit

Talking of organising myself for things to come, I broke the habit of a lifetime and ordered my Christmas turkey a month in advance. Last year I was in a fearful fankle because I'd left it to the last minute and almost ended up killing an old 'coileach' – cockerel – for Christmas dinner. We used to rear turkeys here for the Christmas market and what a trauchle they were from the moment they arrived as week-old chicks until they were ready for killing. I am quite convinced that there is not one brain cell in their bare wattled head. For example, if there was a sudden summer shower the young turkeys would just stand outside, allow their feathers to become waterlogged, contract pneumonia and die before we'd even noticed it was raining. You see our marketing strategy was for free range fresh turkeys so we couldn't break the Trades Description Act by keeping them inside – even in this backwoods neck of the woods. As they grew bigger they would frequently decide to roost on the corrugated iron roof of the barn and it was considered good sport to climb up on a ladder or paraffin drum, and with the byre brush or stable scraper, see how many birds you could shove off the sloping, slippery roof. The stupid turkeys never once realised that if they used their wings they would have a soft landing.

But it was the week before Christmas that the real stramash would start when there were thirty turkeys to pluck, gut and singe. There was an old bodach, Johnny Grant, living on the next croft to Inchdrein, who was an accomplished fiddler and poultry plucker. He did both to perfection if a supporting dram was offered to pluck faster or give us *The Mason's Apron* at teatime.

'Twas the night before Christmas, and all through the house not a creature was stirring not even a mouse' – and twelve turkeys had to be oven ready for five o'clock! It was a gloomy, snowy day, too cold to work outside so it was decided to pluck hell for leather on the linoleum of the kitchen floor. Johnny, well fortified, was in good 'bon', as they say hereabouts, and in order to keep the plucking pace going, would give us a few renditions of his diddling – any tune he could play on the fiddle he could also diddle.

As the day wore on, with more than a touch of Christmas spirit in the air, the pace of plucking and diddling went wildly adrift. And then the shout went up 'Here's the minister'! In these old croft houses there was only one door, and so, in such cases, when an emergency exit was desirable, you just had to stay and face the music, although in this instance it was the minister who faced the music! There we were sitting in deep litter, naked, white turkey breasts emerging from the feathery understorey, scaly, lifeless feet sticking up here and there like corpses on a battlefield; and two stinking pails of entrails. I won't say anything about the parson's nose because he quickly covered it with a hanky – perhaps he was allergic to feathers!

But the funniest episode of all, looking back on that day, was that Johnny was in charge of singeing the birds after plucking, and, as the minister walked in, Johnny was standing with a large bottle of methylated spirits in his hand – it must have been obvious to the minister looking on at this riotous scene, that strong drink had been taken. I often wonder what he thought as Johnny after all had greeted him fairly reverently, or irreverently, as the case may be; he was in the right department but had elevated the minister somewhat!

So what did we have for Christmas dinner that year – certainly not turkey. We had blackcock and capercaillie. The blackcock, I'll always remember, with its dark outer flesh on the breast under which was succulent white meat. Far off days when both birds were plentiful in our forests and regularly came into our stackyard. Nowadays capers are particularly difficult to see. Last week I saw two females, on my walk to Loch Garten, at the same place three days running, yet in the previous month, on the same walk I didn't see one. Blackcock are easier to see, especially on my moorland common grazing. A strikingly handsome bird, the beauty of the male was further enhanced recently as I stopped the car to watch the frail mist rising on early morning sunbeams. There, in a beautiful poise of light, an ebony, aristocratic blackcock viewed the new day from his heathery kingdom.

Much more common this year has been that delightful bird of twilight time, the woodcock. Out at dusk for a walk with the dogs, we disturbed five feeding along the damp roadside edges. I also often see them in boggy areas of birch scrub. We used to eat woodcock regularly, in autumn, on Fair Isle, when they passed through on their southerly migration from Scandinavia. Hundreds arrived with the thrushes and the men of the isle traditionally shot many, sending them to London and Paris markets. It was a much looked forward to event, 'woodcock time' and keenly contested. My old friend George Stout claimed to have shot 101 birds with 99 cartridges. I wonder if he ever claimed the bottle of Bols gin on offer to any one able to prove that they had shot two woodcock with a right and a left barrel. From what I can remember of the islanders' marksmanship, I think they were probably eligible for quite a few crates of gin!

Annie Cameron

They said, when they took Annie to hospital, that she'd never come back; the wind was against the sun and that was a bad sign. The wind was from the west that day and the sun travelled against it setting with a faint rosy bloom behind the Pityoulish hills. Last Saturday we buried Annie in Abernethy churchyard.

Annie Cameron had lived nearly all her eighty-eight years in this township. She became part of the ancient Cameron family whose ancestors originated in Lochaber. A tiny, sprite of a woman, she contributed gallantly to the life and work of the croft without complaint. She often told me, in her latter years, of those early days, her pawky humour often taking the form of rhymes. Dedication was the hallmark of her family, whether it was on the land, with animals or the church. She slipped out of her mortal coat with no struggle whatsoever and there was just a small measure of grief in her passing. But a large crowd of neighbours, crofters, villagers, grocers and postmen, who had known Annie through her long life, paid their last respects. I felt a real touch of sadness as her great nephew piped a lament at her graveside for often in earlier times he and Annie would have some flying, verbal battles about staying up to watch television. But then how could she understand the predilection of the young for cartoons and American cops; Annie had seen five monarchs on the throne of Britain from Edward VII to Elizabeth II. When Annie was growing up in the early 1900s women didn't have the vote, old age pensions were being introduced to the country, vitamins were discovered and Peary reached the North Pole. Sadly Annie leaves a bachelor son, himself a pensioner – what is to become of our shrinking township?

It has been a silent, still time this first month of winter. Never before have I known such a motionless period of weather, with rainfall being well below average. Here on the croft the water has still not returned to some of the usual wet areas, after the summer drought. Normally these provide sufficient water for the cattle, but unfortunately the present dry situation involves me in a complicated animal movement to the burn every morning which needs just one contrary cow or rebellious calf to cause chaos and a time-wasting rodeo. The trouble is, although I can usually persuade the cows that it's in their best interests to go into the field with the burn, mainly because that's the only place they will find their hay, and to take their brats with them, I'm not quite on chatting terms with the bull and I have to hope his 'follow-the-herd' instinct prevails.

Cats, dogs and ducks

I have to admit to being fonder of dogs than cats, so there appears to be no logic behind the fact that I have two dogs and three cats. There's little prey around for the hunting cat at the moment with the rock-hard ground covered in crisp, lifeless vegetation. Birds, of course, are not allowed on the menu in this establishment, so they plead with me for food, by various means from leg rubbing to persistent, penetrating yowling which makes the hackles on the collie's back stand up like a scrubbing brush. Perhaps Ailean nan Creach – Alan of the Spoils – had the right idea as far as cats were concerned. I'll start with the end of the story.

Near the east end of Loch Laggan lie the venerable ruins of St. Kenneth's chapel, attached to which is a curious tradition regarding the building of the church. It was built by Alan Cameron of the Lochiel family. Alan of the Spoils was a noted freebooter and cattle reiver, but his luck ran out when he started experiencing one disastrous raid after the other and in order to counteract his run of bad luck he decided to seek the help of 'the other world'. There was a celebrated witch in his neighbourhood called Gorm Shuil – blue-eyed – who was at the top of her profession being able to transform herself and others into hares or crows, raise gales and blizzards and perform other equally necessary tasks. She told Alan to take a cat, who along with a servant went to a corn kiln at Torcastle, near Spean Bridge. The cat was tied to a spit and the servant started to roast it alive over a slow fire. As soon as the cat started screeching in agony a whole troop of cats gathered to attempt its rescue, but Alan kept them at bay. 'That is a bad way to treat a cat,' screamed the cats. But Alan gave no orders to the servant to stop. Then a huge one-eyed tom cat called Cam Dubh came forward and scolded Alan for his cruelty saying that his misfortunes were all due to his wickedness in stealing from his neighbours and to atone for his sins he must build seven churches. 'If you do not halt immediately, Cluasa Leabhra mo bhrathair, my brother with the long, hanging ears will take such vengence that you will never again receive mercy from the Lord,' warned Cam Dubh.

So sobering was the effect on Alan that he immediately ordered the release of the cat and lost no time in departing before the dreaded Cluasa Leabhra arrived. The seven churches were built before Alan died – one of them is St. Kenneth's chapel at Laggan and another is my family church at Cille Choirill, in Brae Lochaber.

*   *   *   *

Last week was a difficult week if you were a dog trying to bury a bone. We had -15.8 C ground frost one night which turned the earth to iron and left no safe depository for a half-gnawed knuckle bone. After much frantic to-ing and fro-ing to formerly successful vaults, and with jaws exhausted with their heavy hoard, the spaniel had to compromise and hide rather than bury the bone between the grain shed and the old chicken coup. She emerged from the interment looking fairly dissatisfied, a point further emphasised when the collie appeared next morning with the aforementioned bone, the location of which was obviously a piece of cake.

However, they say every dog has its day and the spaniel, who has been too well brought up to show any pique, especially at a 'worker' bringing in a grimey knuckle bone, decided to better her basket-fellow's perform-ance. She borrowed some booty, I assume from the cats, and presented it to me, with what can only be described as a smug expression. It was a weasel. It was frozen solid, of course, and had been neatly nipped in the

neck as the weasel is used to doing to others. A fearsome wee hunter, the weasel is not often beaten and is only rarely killed by other hunters. Perhaps mother cat Lucy's condition – she is thyrotoxic and losing her fur – caused her to become a savage killer, unafraid of any beast, even one with a reputation like the weasel.

Apart from being dry and clean, there is not much else to favour frosty weather. My ducks find it painful and uncomfortable, their bright orange feet contrasting vividly with the glacial whiteness of the snow. Every yard or so they collapse on their feet as the cold becomes unbearable and they cocoon them in the warm feathery down of their belly to bring them back to life. Most of their day is spent in the dusty depths of the old peat shed, or if the sun shines, they will bask by the bales in the dutch barn.

It has been an odd week for ordinary animals. I was alerted when the cats stopped pestering me for food and actually wanted out instead of sleeping on the ironing. I followed them as they skimmed across the ice into the old cart shed where they were only half way through a huge rabbit. It's unusual for them to catch a rabbit at this time of year but there are a lot around even during the day. My neighbour on the hill tells me that the ground is moving with rabbits round his steading – a bad sign weatherwise according to him. Mind you, the day he doesn't come up with a 'bad sign' at some natural phenomenon will indeed be a 'bad sign'.

When the change in the weather came it happened quite suddenly, not long after the new day had established itself. One moment the landscape was static, trees crystallized in the immobile grip of a hard frost, pools imprisoned and lifeless under icy shade and animals and birds sluggish and bored at the prospect of another day of thin air and survival rations. The rise in temperature touched the birches first; in seconds they had changed from Arctic white to cloudy grey to dark burgundy, their branches decked out in glittering droplets of moisture. They shook themselves in the gentle wind leaving 'dotty' patterns on the snow. The distant grey forest slowly shed its frosty film and gradually regained its regal green image. The bird table became an unruly playground as obstreperous bluetits dared to question the authority of the bullying great tits. A robin, perched on the proverbial spade handle, wondered if it was perhaps premature to probe for a worm. Melting snow swelled the puddles on the frozen ground and my scatty ducks skittered across the treacherous surface to the icy bliss of a pool of water. They ducked and dived with great frivolity, they preened and plucked with fevered gaiety, they quacked with genuine hilarity. The lethargic ewes of yesterday were up and away to the forest to nip heather shoots and fussily pick over blaeberry leaves. The cows, deciding not to do anything rash, finished their hay knowing full well that uneaten hay means a cut in supplies next time round.

Before I can sit back and draw breath the forecasters are promising us blizzards and gales with roads blocked and appreciable falls of snow even at low levels. I hot foot it into Grantown to stock up on essential items in case 'the storm' comes and the roads are indeed blocked. The talk in the shops is of the weather with everybody buying two of everything, 'Oh, yes', they said, 'this is going to be an old fashioned winter, just what we are used to here – hard frosts and deep snow.' They rubbed their hands almost gleefully at the thought of meeting this monster blizzard head on.

The morning brought grittily laden sleet showers – bone chilling and very wet. The cows looked miserable and I trauchled with hay an extra 300 yards to feed them in shelter. The sheep erupted from the cover of juniper, like Elijah when he hid under a juniper bush to escape the cruel persecution of King Ahab and the wicked Queen Jezebel. Despite the prickles, the sheep, like the prophet, find the juniper with its gnarled spreading branches excellent shelter, the fallen needles making a good, dry bed.

The forecast was wrong. No great wind came striding over the tree tops of our forest. The trees stirred and sighed, louder and louder, but not stronger and stronger. The sound stayed like background music, the song for that day. It brought no snow to encapsulate and silently steal away our landscape; instead the sweet song of a nervous great tit floated thinly about the forest talk. Not to be outdone my 'mimic' starling responded with a few bars of a black-headed gull which surprised me so much I was almost reaching for the plough.

A lowly cattle shed

There was even a star over the stable at midnight on Christmas Eve as I went out to check the cow. In the late afternoon April gave notice that she was going to calve before morning, and in order to make life easier for man and beast, we put her into the old stable. A cow quite happy to be inside if there is a full heck of hay and a bucket of goodies at intervals, she sniffed, approved and got down to the basic business of eating. At midnight she lay, chewing the cud, unworried and calm in a bed of golden straw, her huge, soft eyes questioning my intrusion while checking my hands for a bucket. As I looked at her, relaxed and warm in the old stable, a roaring wind came galloping in from the west, tormenting the corrugated iron roof and violently rattling the loose skylight. But inside all was calm, all was peace. And I thought about the morning with all my family at home for Christmas, and neighbours invited for Christmas dinner, too. I decided to go to bed and leave April, with a dozen births to date, to get on with it.

On Christmas morning, in that lowly cattle shed, we had a new born calf. It lay peacefully curled up in deep straw, unaware of everything except the soft rumbling from its mother. April, as ever, looked for a bucket — she got three, in fact — two of water to quench her raging thirst and a congratulatory one of bruised barley. Her new calf was a heifer. It was an unusual cinnamon colour all over but with her mother's large, warm Jersey eyes. Hopefully, the Jersey genes will go no further than that as the rangy frame of that breed detracts from a good calf. On the other hand, you can't beat them for the quantity and quality of milk they produce, and as I looked at April's udder, I thought for the umpteenth time that she could easily rear two calves on her milk yield. If only I were organised and could think of locating another calf to synchronise with April's confinement at the same time as mending the Christmas tree lights, cleaning the chimney, remembering where I had hidden presents and meeting endless trains, planes and buses!

Having broken the glad tidings to my still slumbering household, I put the calf up to see that she was sucking properly and to check April's udder. Once on her feet I could see she was a strong and remarkably solid calf. I dragged myself away from the nativity scene to cope with turkey and Christmas presents. After breakfast the calf was admired by everyone and there was much animated discussion about what to call her. Suggestions ranged from Noelle to Madge but, as Boxing Day is the feast of St. Stephen, we decided to call the calf Stephanie, to be shortened to Stephie.

*   *   *   *

When my neighbour on the hill returned home the other night from his festive township travels, warmer inside than out, he found a note on his door which read – 'There's a bottle of whisky in the chimney for you. S.Claus'. Never one to miss a chance, whether it's when the keeper is off to Inverness with his wife for a day's shopping or the chance of liquid nourishment from some mythical character. Sharper than anyone when it comes to finding the gold (liquor) at the end of the rainbow, he went immediately to the old broken chimney pot lying at the barn door and sure enough there was the bottle of whisky with a note from an old friend wishing him a Happy New Year!

JANUARY

Flights of fancy

It was Hoagy Carmichael who sang about the 'Buttermilk Sky', leaning on a five bar gate, enthusing at the beauty of the sky while waiting to meet his loved one. It's not often you see that delicate colour as it only occurs under certain conditions such as were present last weekend. It is most often seen in the hour preceding sunset before the stronger colours of the setting sun dominate the sky. It appears as a wide band of pale sky between the horizon and the cloud cover and you have to look for a moment or two before you can appreciate the special quality of the buttermilk sky as at a first glance it appears to be just a wishy washy blue. If you persevere you will see the hint of green, shades of blue and creamy tones – a delicate mixture of the more gentle celestial colours. It is, of course, the same colour, exactly, as the liquid left at the bottom of the churn after the butter has been separated from the milk. All too soon the ebullient bands of sunset take over and the fragile buttermilk sky has slipped away. An illusive colour, eminently suited to a tender love song.

I have never known a winter in which we have been better blessed with so many spectacular sunrises and sunsets. Driving home from Inverness last week through a spellbinding setting sun, I felt I just had to stop on the Slochd to absorb its beauty as well as for the safety of other road users. There were long, thin trails of cloud in endless layers above the horizon and as the sun set each layer turned into gleaming gold ribbons arranging and rearranging themselves in spangling banners. Sunrises have been more subdued, more definite in pattern, subtle in expression, like comparing watercolours to oils. This morning frothy blobs of white cloud turned to a blanket of pink candy floss as the sun rose steadily behind the distant green forest. As it trudged up the Shepherd's Hill and peeped over the shoulder, winking at birches, sparkling in pools, the clouds merged, and leaving their rosy bed behind, drifted off to cap some lofty peaks, perhaps.

*   *   *   *

We are in the middle of January, and as I look out at our hills, the highest of which is 2,700 feet, there is not the tiniest patch of snow. While I sympathise with the winter sports operators in our area, everyday that goes by without snow is a bonus. But to have a temperature of + 14C in January is bizarre. This point was underlined recently when I had my heifer, Angie, in the byre overnight while waiting on her to calve. In the morning Angie's coat was sparkling with sweat. This happened on three consecutive mornings and I decided that this probably wasn't very good for the cow. Despite it being her first calf she gave birth outside on a sunny hillock, without problems. Keeping cattle inside in winter, when the weather is mild and moist, can lead to problems, not the least of which is pneumonia. The cattleman from the neighbouring estate tells me that they keep all their stock outside in winter as they have plenty of shelter and pointing to a plantation said 'A roaring blizzard wouldn't blow a match out in there'.

Driving into Grantown during the last few weeks, I have, several times, seen a stoat prancing playfully around the roadside dyke at Culreach. A few days later I was thrilled to see a milky white stoat in shining ermine ripple along the top of the dyke, his black tipped tail flicking pertly over mossy stones. The moult to white begins in November and may be completed in seventy-two hours or take several weeks. The change back to brown can be equally dramatic or prolonged. Sadly, either in daytime playtime or nocturnal hunt, one of the stoats, a brown one, crossed the evil, black tarmac and was killed. He lay in the gritty gutter, his creamy belly stained with grey, oily water. This ebullient little hunter, with his wall of death performances, was dead and I was instantly sad.

*   *   *   *

The old people are taken, my neighbour believes, when the leaves are falling or the buds forming. Last autumn we lost two once doughty old ladies; Annie's frail spark of life extinguished like a puff of wind blowing out a candle, and Dorothy, robust but paralysed, went gently enough too. They too knew those same sunrises and sunsets. Their loss to our small community was real indeed, like a piece of the Shepherd's Hill breaking off and crumbling away to dust. They have gone now but the hills and forests, the bogs and birches, streams and sunsets endure. A favourite American writer, Edward Hoagland puts it rather better, 'Wildness is permanence because it is unaltered, an infinity of particulars, which are changing only very slowly, without special reference to man'.

*   *   *   *

They say the climate in southern California is palpable; a commodity that can be labelled, priced and marketed without fear of it changing or a law suit being taken out for incorrect trades description. It is consistent, predictable and possibly monotonous. They have two seasons a year; the wet and the dry. Last week we had two seasons in two days here in Strathspey.

The snow came on the heels of the gale which had come galloping in from the west at great speed flattening slender saplings, shaking the roots of gigantic green pines and spitefully tormenting loose corrugated roofing on the old steading. In the morning the hills were dark and drenched with westerly rains; a blue daylight pervaded the scene, the sky being neither grey or blue. Like dark-eyed daughters the hills looked down on Mother Earth; the atmosphere felt burdened with elemental force. The old folks would have looked philosophical and said 'Aye, the glass is not looking good, there's a change on the way'.

The change came like a theatrical production with a fast moving white curtain falling on the present stage, dimming daylight and cancelling the backdrop. Swirling snowflakes filled the air, rushing horizontally past the window, carried along with fearful pace. Occasionally the gale would pause, appear to gasp for breath causing the snow to go spiralling skywards. In two hours we had two inches of snow, boiling black clouds brewing up more behind the mountains. The darkness which had been with us most of the day intensified to night; it stopped snowing but blew harder than ever, paring down sounds so that cattle roaring in the field were almost inaudible.

During the night the cloud conspiracy behind the mountains had been rumbled. In the morning the snow had melted into the brown shadows of moor and mountain. The wind, while present, was only gently in attendance, barely ruffling white fleeces. The sun, almost late arriving on this balmy scene, turned dull mosses vibrant and dour birch branches to burgundy. By midday the temperature was +13C and we were tidying up the old stackyard in our shirt sleeves. Windows were opened to allow in some 'fresh air'. If I'd the time, I reckon I could have seen the grass grow. Chaffinches and yellowhammers opted for the outdoor pool and bathed busily, plucking and preening, in a puddle by the gate. With wing bars and tails feathers immaculately groomed they crossed the road for a meal of yarrow and fat hen seeds. My bees stretched their wings, took a flight of fancy and a sup of cool fresh water in pleasant mid-winter sunshine. Only twelve hours ago a blizzard had raged, leaving the countryside cheerless and inhospitable.

The other evening I was watching a film on television in which the heroine saved the day, and herself, by knocking out her assailant with the stiletto heel of her shoe. A similar incident happened in this township about three hundred years ago and to this day a cairn marks the spot where the lady slayed her kidnapper.

Barbara Grant of Rynettin was a lady of great beauty and charm and had many admirers, the most ardent and persistent of which was Donald Cameron from Lochaber. Barbara spurned his advances and pledged her troth to Seumas MacPherson, a local lad. But Donald Cameron was a ruthless man and decided to use force where soft words had failed. On the Sunday before Barbara's wedding to MacPherson, the family went to church while Barbara stayed at home. Cameron and his men invaded the croft and Barbara was abducted along with as much booty as could be removed. Barbara did not accept defeat easily and along the trail surreptiously tore strands of wool from her shawl and dropped them onto the track to mark her direction. But the trail of wool did not satisfy her determination to outwit her kidnappers, and carefully removing one strongly heeled shoe, and fixing her eye on a point behind the ear of the man who was leading the pony to which she was strapped, she took aim and hit the Cameron man with such force that he fell to the ground stone dead. Catching the reins and swinging the pony round, Barbara galloped off leaving the Lochaber men in great confusion. Soon Barbara met a strong party of Tulloch men following her trail of wool and after joyful greetings, she went back to Rynettin while her family pursued the Cameron kidnappers. They were overtaken in Badenoch and severely routed by the men of Tulloch who came home in triumph with all their booty. Needless to say Barbara's wedding was celebrated with much jubilation.

Snowdrifts and little people

Being one of the little people, I had great problems last week walking through snow drifts, two feet deep, covering the croft. That left only three feet of me above the snow line which meant that my wellies soon became packed with snow, ankle and calf immobile in an icy grip, or should I say drip. With leaden legs and possible trench foot, I stumbled and tumbled across the fields of flying snow like a Canadian trapper returning from a hunting trip. What I need for these desperate days of drifts is a pair of puttees. I know, for I still have the Strathspey Herald, that they were 2/6 a pair in 1928 from MacGregors, the Saddlers in Grantown but I doubt whether Marks and Spencers stock them today. A puttee is a strip of woollen cloth which is wrapped from ankle to knee effectively keeping you warm and dry. They were used extensively in the First World War. Gaiters, I suppose, are the modern equivalent but I find them an awful footer especially as manufacturers appear to ignore the little people. Last week I had to resort to waterproof trousers which certainly kept me dry, but left me hot, bothered and irritable – they are much too noisy to be wearing in the countryside. I don't want to miss the hilarity of the green woodpecker, the absurd petulance of the cock pheasant flushed from the

birches or the cackling of an eireag as she lays her first egg in a secret dark hollow in the bales.

An old neighbour from the edge of the forest, who is no longer around, made his own puttees from the lightweight sacking of corn bags. I can clearly remember him turning up at the croft, legs tightly wrapped in puttees, picking his way carefully through snow and ice, the fiddle case under his arm, for an evening of tunes. Having dispensed good music and good crack, and absorbed strong drink, Johnny would leave his fiddle at the croft for safekeeping, and make his way home, somewhat unsteadily, on puttee-wrapped legs. Everytime I hear *The Conundrum* or *Sprig o' Ivy* played on a fiddle a nostalgic and vivid picture of Johnny comes immediately to mind. Neighbours are more than just the bodach or caillaich on the hill. They sometimes don't say much, or they tell you the same thing each visit, but their permanence is precious, the threads of our lifes intertwining affectionately today, the broken threads of yesterday deep, treasured memories.

Last week I just managed to beat the blizzard home arriving limp and exhausted after a nasty journey over the Slochd in dimming daylight and swirling snow. The snow was already drifting on the croft forming tiny cornices along the field edge, and with incredible speed developing into deep drifts of powdery snow. The sheep I hoped had made for the shelter of the huge spreading pines in the forest. I never saw them and assumed they were safe. You can usually rely on animals to do the sensible thing in bad weather; it's we humans who are unpredictable and stupid. The cows, too, had vanished, deserting their usual feeding place which was being strafed by heavy punching snow showers. I shouted to them and they caught my call as it was being tossed through the thumping wind and snow. They, of course, were in the most sheltered part of the field, under a slope of rowans, below the birches; grey shapes in a white world encapsulated in the demonic power of the blizzard. The driving snow all but closed my eyes, icy flakes clinging to my eyelashes, clawing at my face with a stinging power which left my cheeks feeling scarred. Falling in the door I left the weather to show off its supremacy without any argument from me.

I woke to silence; a sinister, heavy stillness which made opening the curtains feel like playing Russian roulette. What would I find? The snow lay deep. It was falling in a dense, determined way as if productivity had to be doubled in a day. By midday the snow had reached that target. My neighbour on the hill appeared at the door dressed surprisingly in a suit, collar and tie. Not exactly appropriate gear for present weather conditions and I can guarantee he is not an unpredictable stupid human being! Peeling off the outer layer revealed a black tie. He'd been on his way to a funeral in Nethy Bridge and his lift hadn't materialised due to a blocked road, and, seeing my smoke, he gave me a call. We discussed everything from his black tie which he bought for his grandfather's funeral in 1938 to the Invergordon Mutiny. Despite being born and bred on a hill farm, and having lived there for over sixty years, he is passionately interested in the sea and the Navy and has a store of facts associated with both, which I find astonishing and admirable. We shared a boozy lunch of toasted cheese and a can of stout and talked of the weather; awful weather, great company.

Next day with eighteen inches of snow on our road, I have to help dig Eric the Red (post van) out of a drift. How cheerful and amiable everyone is in these days of harsh weather. The countryside has an artificial, synthetic look though, bald, shiny, perfectly sculpted in white; no brutal colours, no ugly shapes. Green forests are arranged tastefully in the background, dark, delicate birches filling in the gaps while this whole arrangement is set off against a cornflower blue sky. Huge white shoulder pads of snow overhang buildings making me duck as I go into the byre to feed an old ewe who has come in to graze in these bone-chilling conditions. The dogs, short of exercise because of my difficulty in walking and lack of puttees, decide to have a final frolic in the snow. As I stand at the door to call them I hear a gentle tap, tap and a puff of wind caresses my face. The snow is dripping off the roof and the thaw has come. After a heavy fall of snow a thaw is a messy process. Snow and mud turn to clarty gruel underfoot while puddles look like brown milk shakes.

There is small talk at my bird table once more as the tits reappear from their forest storm isolation. Brazen jackdaws banter confidently a few feet from the cattle, sounding like a group of quarrelsome schoolchildren. How the cows tolerate these wisecracking, grey suited, black-capped gentlemen, I just don't know.

Most people in Strathspey, from farmers to fishermen, were delighted to see such a heavy fall of snow. The lack of snow last year had a disastrous effect on the salmon run in the Spey during the 1988 season. Now that there will be snow melt this year it should mean a good run of spring fish for the opening of the season in mid-February. At least half a dozen farmers that I know of were without their usual supply of water up until this week. My neighbour's supply only came back the day of the thaw and I remember being at his clipping in August and having to go to the burn for water. Fortunately, he's a bachelor with no automatic washing machine to worry about. He uses a bucket, a washing board, Sunlight soap and dries his washing on a line in the barn. His water table should rise considerably after the snow — he has an eight foot drift at the end of his steading.

As you may have gathered I have a certain affiliation to little people and music, so I'll tie these two threads together and tell about an incident which took place just over the Shepherd's Hill from here in Glenmore. It involved a famous hunter, Robin Oig, a son of the Stewarts of Kincardine. Returning from a hunting trip one day he met a party of fairies on the march with their pipers. The music was the finest he'd ever heard and he listened entranced. As they passed he noticed that the pipes were of silver, sparkling with jewels. Throwing his bonnet among the little folks he shouted — 'Mine to you, yours to me' — and snatched the pipes. The fairy procession moved on and Robin Oig hurried home with the precious pipes hidden under his plaid. But when he got home and reached triumphantly for the pipes he had nothing but an empty puff-ball and a spike of grass!

FEBRUARY

Whales

Whales have been on this planet longer than we have; it's a sad fact that man, as a species, may outlive them for we have pushed them to the very edge. Extinction for some types is a probability rather than a possibility. So it was with great sadness and yet some excitement, that I was taken to see a dead sperm whale on the sand dunes behind the Culbin Bar on the Moray Firth.

It had probably died or been killed at sea and how long it had floated before beaching is difficult to say. Despite a huge gash being torn in its back by a ship's propeller, it still looked dignified in death. I found it a most heart-rending sight – its gentleness still apparent, its vulnerability most palpable.

The scientific name for the sperm whale is *Physeter macrocephalus* which comes from the Greek for 'big head'. But the English name has a different derivation. The presence in the whale's head of a reservoir of clear liquid which sets to a solid white wax on cooling, led to analogies with semen and the name spermaceti, literally whale semen, hence sperm whale.

The sperm whale beyond Culbin Bar was a male and nearly fifty foot long, although they can grow to sixty-five foot. The profile of the sperm whale is unmistakable with an enormous head, blunt snout and relatively small underslung jaw. There is no dorsal fin as such but we noticed a distinct dorsal bump halfway along the back. The tail flukes are broad and powerful, and their size is greater than in any other whale, providing rapid acceleration. The entire skin surface looked to me like the worn tread on an old tyre, slightly corrugated and blistered in places. The colour of our whale was steely grey but apparently as sperm whales grow older they become paler or develop white patches. In 1957 a pure white adult male, exactly like the mythical Moby Dick, was taken in Japanese waters and was considered not to be an albino.

We noticed that the blow hole was situated well to the left of centre and it's said that the first exhalation after a deep dive is like an explosion which can be heard nearly a mile away. These whales regularly dive to 3,500 feet but can go down to 10,000 feet as the presence of sea-bed dwelling sharks in a whale's stomach has proved. Their diet consists mainly of squid, eating up to a ton a day. Also appearing on their menu are lobsters, skate, jellyfish, cod and fourteen foot sharks. Accidentally included have been boots, wire, buckets and the ubiquitous plastic bag. We counted 23 pairs of conical teeth on the lower jaw and you could easily see that they fitted snugly into sockets on the upper palate.

Throughout the world sperm whale strandings are not infrequent and often involve whole herds. A whale expert from New Zealand writes that mass strandings usually mean the beaching of a close-knit harem herd which begins with just one individual coming ashore. This whale emits a loud and sustained distress call which is picked up by the rest of the herd, who mill about distractedly offshore. Eventually another whale will detach itself and become stranded. This pattern repeats itself until the entire herd is helpless on the shore. In 1974 a group of seventy-two sperm whales were stranded on a beach in New Zealand.

Sperm whales tend to be aggressive only when protecting their young but I did read that in 1820 an American ship called the Essex rammed a large male basking on the surface of the Pacific Ocean. Much disturbed, the whale hit the ship several times until it sank. Only one lifeboat with three crew reached the coast of Peru to tell the tale. But man's influence on the sperm whale has been far more dramatic; in 1963 the world catch of the species was over 30,000. Since then controls and common sense have reduced the slaughter.

In exactly the same place, on Culbin Bar, just over one hundred years ago, a fifty foot blue whale was beached. The Moray Firth appears to be an important site for beached whales. A few years ago, but nearer to Inverness, I saw a Sowerby's whale, one of the beaked whale species. And it was as a result of a stranding in 1800 on the Moray Firth that this whale was first identified and described. James Brodie of Brodie collected and preserved the skull and beak of the dead whale. This came to the notice of a travelling naturalist and painter, James Sowerby, who made a detailed portrait of the whale which, ever afterwards, was known as Sowerby's whale.

Capercaillie count

Last weekend I was involved with another species which, while not close to extinction, is having problems sustaining a buoyant population. The capercaillie, our largest game bird, is now more difficult to see than an osprey. The RSPB had invited foresters, landowners, conservationists and crofters to their caper count on one of their forest reserves. A motley crew of brown people turned up, with beards and binoculars, gaiters and gortex. Crofters were easily identified by their turned down wellies, imitation thermal jackets, bare red hands and collies. Nell, my collie, was embarrassed by an odious male pointer who behaved like a lager lout and sniffed so much that she spent most of the day sitting down to avoid any further wounding of her sensitive personality. At midday, soup, sausage rolls, tea and drams refuelled most counters but like finely tuned powerful engines, some folks needed more fuel than others. My neighbour on the hill, cromag in one hand, bottle in the other, was last to leave the canteen, the thought of half full whisky bottles left unattended, causing an internal conflict, externally visible. However, on his way again, fired by the abdominal combustion, he beat his way through the old wood of Caledon like the horse of the woods itself, the capercaillie. He is a strong, steady walker, and despite being over sixty, has the stamina of a man half his age. Mind you if your early training involved carrying a stag on your back in a blizzard from the foot of Bynack to Tulloch then you, too, would be tough and resilent. At the end of the day forty-eight capers were seen, exactly the same number as last year which was encouraging considering that they had a very disappointing breeding season with just 0.6 chicks to every female bird. In the 60s there were nearly 10,000 pairs of capers in the Highlands and Grampian; now there are just 1000 pairs. Modern forestry practices are mostly to blame with their dense plantations and high fences into which capers fly. My neighbour left his cromag in my care, as, with 'Grouse' as opposed to caper in one hand, he went off to reminisce with cronies on the great days of caper shooting as opposed to caper counting!

There are only two species of capercaillie in the world and himself with the well-stamped passport has seen them both. The western caper as it is sometimes called, can basically be seen at the bottom of the garden but he saw the smaller, darker, black-billed caper in the forests of northern Mongolia. He is probably the only person in Scotland to have seen both species of caper and certainly the only person to have seen both and eaten one!

The perpetual roar of that mighty wind has, at times, been hard to bear this week as it batters and tramples the countryside, howling down chimneys, bruising my solitude, disturbing my sleep. It has ripped the corrugated iron roof off both the stick and peat shed, blown down tenacious birch trees and scattered hay as soon as you put it out. Partner in crime has been the rain, heavy, punishing, bullying showers showing no respite, no reprieve; shelter for beasts was sacramental. But at eight hundred foot above sea level, I was blessed compared to some. My neighbour at the end of the forest, next to the Spey, had to rescue his wintering sheep by canoe borrowed from the local outdoor centre. You live by a river all your life and you think you know it, its moods, its habits, its style. But a river will show you it's a living, working part of this planet as capable as we are of behaving badly, causing disaster and destroying life.

Lawless animals – goats and men

When I was a little girl I used to travel to Inverness perhaps four times a year; now I am in Inverness at least four times a week. But in those early days the half-way highlight was to spot the German's head, carved out of the rock, at the Slochd. It was less dangerous to stop then, or travel slowly, consequently we nearly always saw that distinctive German helmet and sharp nose. I still cast my eyes over the rocky screes, but now it's in the hope of seeing the wild goats, which quite frequently are browsing between bare boulders. Last week I saw three scraggy coated nannies sheltering under a rocky overhang, with their contented tiny kids.

It's odd that our wild goats have never evolved so that they might have their young at a more equable time of year. They give birth now as do the goats of the Middle East from whom our wild goats are descended.

It is thought our goats, which were originally Persian wild goats, first came to Britain in herds driven across the dry English Channel before we quite literally broke away from Europe. These beasts became domesticated, but as goats have a tendency to run wild, a feral population became established in the country and it's from that population that our Highland wild goats are descended.

I always think goats are more attractive to look at than boring white sheep, with their black and white, or brown and white or all black coats. If you ever get close enough to a goat you will see they have funny eyes – sort of sceptical, arrogant and definitely intolerant. I have never felt completely at ease with goats, wild or domesticated, and always get the feeling that the goats are controlling the situation and are likely to show you so whenever they please. In short, they can be the most obstinate and lawless of animals. My mother tells of a vigilant goat they had on their croft in Brae Lochaber, who as soon as a door was left open, would be in eating everything from sugar to soap. This nanny could also negotiate the steep narrow staircase, up and down, as if it were a slope of boulders. Norman MacCaig, too, has personal experience of goats:

> The steepest thatch of barn or byre is pavement to his foot, the last,
> loved rose, a prisoner to his snatch.

Goats can survive in the harshest conditions on mountain tops eating lichen and moss, but if given the chance can be alarmingly destructive. I discovered this rather far flung example in an old book the other day. It concerns St. Helena in the south Atlantic.

When it was discovered by the Portuguese in 1502 the island was covered by luxuriant forests and a rich variety of 'peculiar' plants. Goats were introduced in 1513 and multiplied rapidly. Soon native plants and even the tropical forest began to disappear, although in 1709 the indigenous ebony tree was still abundant enough to allow it to be used as a fuel for burning lime. With the enormous increase in goat numbers new forest growth was severely limited, and when the older trees had eventually all been cut down by man, it was realised in 1810, that the primaeval forest had gone, leaving no successors to take their place. St. Helena, which was once a precious oasis for tropical plant life, set in the midst of the Atlantic, had become a barren rocky waste.

In the windswept hostility of these foothills on which the croft sits, we are not lucky enough to have any really early spring flowers. But if you visit the softer pastures of Easter Ross and the Black Isle, you will see at the moment, growing in selected, secluded haunts, butterbur. When they first push through the soil they look like slightly flushed button mushrooms but later on tasselled flowers make butterbur look more like some dwarf pink conifers. They are a valuable source of early nectar and in Scandinavia are often deliberately planted round beehives. Only the flowers appear at the moment and it's not until the late summer that the leaves start to crowd the damp waysides. The leaves are huge and could easily be used as a makeshift umbrella to shelter you from heat or rain. It's from the use of the leaves that butterbur gets its name, for it was used to wrap butter to keep it cool in the days before cold storage. The leaves have a lint-like furriness and are pliable and thick enough to cushion the butter from bruising and to soak up any seepage or melting. They remind me of vine leaves and are easier to use to wrap up left-overs or cheese than cling film!

*   *   *   *

One of the major tasks on the croft this year will be to repair a fairly extensive march fence which, just over two hundred years ago, caused one man to murder another.

Around 1772 two neighbouring farmers, John MacGibbon and John Grant, fell out over this particular march fence. It was May time and John MacGibbon was mending the fence to protect some reclaimed land on which he was to plant potatoes. Grant came along and accused him of ill-treating his sheep and soon a violent argument got up in what is now an outpost of the township. MacGibbon, fed up with Grant's insults, took up his gun meaning to scare rather than hurt the young man. Unfortunately Grant was fatally wounded and despite desperate efforts to stop the bleeding, he died. MacGibbon was immediately charged with murder but couldn't be found and it is believed he'd fled the country.

Some thirty years later a local man went out for an evening stroll while serving with the army in Holland. He came upon a group of men working on an embankment and much to his surprise one of them spoke to him in Gaelic. 'Where do you come from?' he asked. The answer was 'Scotland'. 'What part?' 'Strathspey'. The name obviously brought heart-felt memories to the old man and with a trembling lip he said, 'Am bheil na tre chraobhan chaorain fathasd ann Buchonich?' 'Are there three rowan trees still at Buchonich?' 'Yes, they are standing there yet,' replied MacQueen. At that moment the drum beat and MacQueen had to hurry back to camp. It is believed that this poor exiled Highlander was, in fact, John MacGibbon.

Robert Frost's poem 'Mending Wall' is for me a lovely sideways look at fencing. It tells of two neighbours who have joint responsibility for mending a march wall in the spring.

I let my neighbour know beyond the hill;
And on a day we meet to walk the line
And set the wall between us once again.

One asks the other why they need a wall or a fence when there are no cows to keep in, or out, but his recalcitrant neighbour always replies :

Good fences make good neighbours.

He's right, too.

MARCH

Exuberant spring

Part of the view from the croft is now owned by an American. This gentleman recently bought the small Scots pine plantation to secure the valuable seed source. The seeds from here will be exported to Michigan, where the climate is very like that of Strathspey, and where they will be grown on for the Christmas tree market. The demand for pure Scots pine seed is increasing and present sources were becoming so unreliable and inconsistent that my American neighbour decided to buy his own Highland forest in what is the present day heartland of the ancient Caledonian pine. He couldn't have chosen a better year to buy for the pine trees this year are hanging heavy with cones. He has employed local men to pick the cones, from which the seed will be extracted by drying them in a kiln. My neighbour on the hill was taken on and not for the first time in his life found himself in an unstable situation. Not that there was strong drink taken but the movement at the top of a pine tree in a westerly gale is quite considerable. It was a turbulent but profitable exercise he told me later with both feet on the ground, and all because Americans like the look and smell of Scots pine Christmas trees.

*   *   *   *

There's nothing pleases a reformed poacher more than being asked to a deer count on the estate and dreaming of what might have been. My neighbour on the hill spent one day last week trudging through high heather and dark forests where he once roamed solitary, silent and stealthily. To control the environmental vandalism caused by red deer in the

Abernethy Forest Nature Reserve requires careful management and culling of the deer and to that end a fairly accurate count is necessary. My neighbour saw few deer, 'a puckle stags', and treated the total figure with a degree of scepticism, reckoning that some folk counted the same beasts three times. The counters, too, were controlled for the day, with whistles in case any of them got lost in the gloomy hollows of Bognacruie. This safety measure was wasted on my neighbour who knew how to get wherever and exactly how long it would take. But then he would, wouldn't he, having spent much time in the past timing a raid to the last minute while the keeper was perhaps away shopping in town with his wife. Some of those who crossed one river too many and ended up in the lonely wastes of the Slaich, were impressed by his doubtful skill.

It's been a week of multitudinous births on the croft — twenty-one lambs and two calves, all hale and hearty, and elating for me. My obsessed silver-backed cow gave birth, as one might have expected, on the 13th day of March, exactly a year to the date on which she calved last year. Not for her the seclusion of a sheltered birch grove away from nosey heifers and curious calves, in which to give birth. She dropped her calf on the bare hillock surrounded by the inquisitive herd, which stood around her like a rugby scrum waiting to form. Looking out of my kitchen window I noticed through umpteen pairs of legs, four very wobbly new limbs, frantically lurching from one warm, wet nose to another while the neurotic mother rushed after the calf, her afterbirth swishing behind her like a bridal train. In one minute flat I shedded the old from the new, sedated the mother with a bucket of bruised barley while her new heifer calf filled her tiny lungs with sweet spring air.

Maggie, on the other hand, gave birth, hid her calf in dry, springy heather and was nonchalantly chewing her cud when found. Her boy is bulky and looks slightly gormless. I never cease to be amazed at the skill with which the cows hide their tiny calves while they go off to feed sometimes half a mile away in the forest. This behaviour is just like that of red and roe deer. Before I sat down to write, Maggie came home without her calf obviously having forgotten where she had left it. She roared for five minutes hoping it might come home itself saving her a trauchle through the bogs looking for it. In the end we had to go and look for it – and Maggie came too. She rushed around here and there looking under spikey junipers and sniffing in heathery hollows. Every now and again she would charge over looking at us with her white-lashed eyes which said 'Have you found him yet'? Eventually his pink nose and soft ginger ears were spotted by my husband on a bed of fresh blaeberry leaves.

I always feel desperately sad when the wind tramples through my crocuses knocking them down with the same evil power with which it disposes of the mighty pine. Some flowers never feel the warmth of our fragile spring sunshine and fade without ever opening their petals. In warm but turbulent conditions last week I watched one of my bees valiantly trying to collect pollen from the golden stamen of a purple petalled crocus. It clung on tenaciously as the wind tossed the flower hither and thither; small trouble for this giant's breath.

Very often simple sights give greatest pleasure. I have been charmed this week by a robin sitting on an arthritic old grey tree stump on which was growing a blithe, sunny daisy; by a pair of oystercatchers their exotic orange bills clamorous against crisp, green grass; by the black-bibbed, jaunty pied wagtail, who sits on my garden fence, makes friends with beast and fowl and who, before flying off perhaps to investigate the gooseberry bush in the old stackyard, chinks merrily – I believe he says – you can come too.

*   *   *   *

Yesterday, I came across some black headed gulls eating a white hare on the Slochd summit. Fifteen years ago this would not have been worthy of a mention but white hares or mountain hares are so scarce that even one killed on the road is something of a tragedy. In days gone by a winter hare shoot was an event, both sporting and social, much looked forward to by crofters, farmers and keepers. My neighbour on the hill went every year to Knockando where maybe 500 hares were shot in one day. Everybody took home as many as they wanted and often the rest were just buried. My old aunt recalls shoots in this area with the white hares moving up the Shepherd's Hill like drifting snow. Despite that slaughter, it is not generally believed that it was responsible for the decline of the white hare. For once I think that two other species, apart from man, can take much of the blame – sheep and red deer. Both have hammered our hills and left much degradation behind them.

Now is the time for the mountain hare's summer coat to begin growing in again. By mid-May it will be a dusky brown colour, but with a slightly grizzled appearance and bluish bloom; ear tips are black but the tail is white in all seasons. Along with the stoat, the mountain hare is the only other British mammal to turn white in winter. The only bird to moult, in tune with its environment, is the ptarmigan. This change of plumage is beautifully described, translated from Gaelic, and collected by Thomas Sinton.

Thou art the feahsome one of the high peaked mountains, in most dainty attire; for whiteness about Candlemas, like the cotton flower. Nor is thy after hue at all less beautiful, – like lichen on the hill ground, streaked with sleat.

*   *   *   *

I've just received my latest dose of advice on diversification; last time it was snails, this time it's angora rabbits. And believe it or not but, you, the tax payer, are paying for me to have this advice. Obviously half a dozen rabbits in a hutch at the bottom of the garden would not be viable, so we are being advised to keep four hundred, shearing them every thirteen weeks and making sure the temperature doesn't rise above 25°C before clipping or below 5° after clipping. It's bad enough when four wily black faced ewes wander into my neighbour's garden, snipping crocus heads and precious alpine plants; sheep, at least, are retrievable. What would be the scenario if four hundred angora rabbits escaped – you certainly couldn't send the collie out to round them up! Even worse – what if the dogs got into the 'hutch' with four hundred long-haired, captive rabbits – it would be worse than a cat among pigeons.

Butterflies and blizzards

It's been a week of butterflies and blizzards; the treasures of spring lay before us one moment to be buried under inches of snow the next. Only last Saturday we were in shirt sleeves ear-marking new lambs while older lambs lay in dry hollows, heads held high absorbing the comforting heat from the sun. Small tortoiseshell butterflies fluttered with airy dalliance in warm sunbeams as noiselessly as rose petals floating to the ground in high summer. They made reconnaisance flights to newly emerged nettles growing belligerently from the ruins of an old stone dyke, storing the information for the day egg laying will begin. But where are they now that we are once more encapsulated in a snowy world which has all but dimmed that golden touch of spring. Their soft velvety wings would become paralysed with cold as the clinging chill of winter settled on their delicate bodies. Hopefully, they would have felt the air turn thin and cold before the heavy snowflakes filled the air and covered the ground. I hope they are snug behind a cobweb curtain in a crack in the barn or perhaps between stone and stall in the stable. Man and beast must be tolerant of spring, this season of promise whose word of honour can be so unreliable, who gambles with our hopes and fears; with butterflies and blizzards.

Two months ago the flooding in the Great Glen and in Strathspey made national headlines. The flooded fields along the Spey are still with us and are no longer news. The devastation of two months ago is daily devastation for the farmers affected. Driving to Grantown-on-Spey the hillocks at Balliefirth stand out in an ocean which once was a river, like newly born volcanic islands. On them are two or three tide marks which is a measure of the ebb and flow of the floods. On a windy day white capped waves crash on their shores and I expect to see a stern trawler or herring drifter come punching through the stormy waters. To me it's like something I have imagined – I still can't quite believe my eyes each time I pass this sea called the Spey. But the birds have been quick to take advantage of this nutritious expanse of water with five hundred assorted ducks dabbling where grass should be growing. Mallard, wigeon and teal are there in high numbers with smaller counts of tufted duck. Plowtering about around the edges and up water-logged ditches are curlew, oystercatcher, lapwing, snipe and redshank. Over one thousand black-headed gulls congregate in large cacophonous flocks bathing exuberantly in this newly formed swimming pool. Soon they take wing, refreshed, to reclaim their nesting territories; white feathers float on grey waters under which the earth is silent.

Are we ourselves not to blame, in part, for this desolation? Have we used and manipulated the land to a point where it is so vulnerable that any deviation of the elements causes destruction? Perhaps a more philosophical rather than a profitable outlook might be the way forward. Thirty years ago, what has happened on the Spey would never have taken place, I was told by a man who lived near the Spey for many years. He said in those days the flood banks were covered in broom, gorse and bushes and the cattle and sheep were never in any danger because they could always seek safety there. These flood banks never eroded because of the bushes. He added that the large ditches were of utmost importance and kept in good order to cope with the flood water when the river was high. Perhaps conditions this year were exceptional but a river is a living, working part of our countryside and if we don't learn its ways, or ignore how it works, we do so at our peril.

How boring life would be if our weather was predictable and the seasons ran true to form. It is seven o'clock in the evening and I have just been out to feed the beasts in warm evening sunshine which is casting long shadows over the sparkling snowy landscape. Where else could you find on a spring evening, four inches of snow, blazing sunshine, a mistle thrush singing and a curlew yodelling; bizarre, wonderful and entertaining. Just below the house we have a green, miry patch which is always open and never freezes as it is the run-off from the well. Being the only fresh ground available this morning an incredible bevy of birds gathered there to feed and preen. The spring water bubbled and sparkled and trickled away through banks of snow to the burn. Here and there crisp green grass islands became a landing stage for spotted songthrushes and starlings while plucky pied wagtails travelled through muddy channels disturbing tasty beetles, perhaps. Chic yellowhammers and chaffinches kept to the snowy sidewalks possibly worried about their bright new spring dress; but my robin adopted his winter pose of sitting on the spade handle in the garden – background, snow of course.

How different was their behaviour last Saturday when newly arrived meadow pipits, spick and span in immaculate stripes, parachuted on open wings from alder trees by the burn in death-defying plunges. An oyster-catcher sitting on the flat calm loch, like a plastic decoy, attempted to swim across, for a giggle, while his mate sat on an old fence post watching him make a fool of himself. Despite being a wader oystercatchers don't have webbed feet and are about as good at swimming as my cats are at the doggy paddle.

A ghillie's story

I used to think my family tree went back a long way – it starts in 1164 – but I recently met an old man in Invergarry who showed me his family tree going back to 732 – that's only about two hundred years after St. Columba arrived on Iona. Jock MacAskill's family were of the MacDonells of Glengarry whose lands once extended from Loch Oich, through Knoydart almost to the western seaboard at Loch Hourn. The Chiefs lived in the now ruined Invergarry Castle until 1746 and Culloden, and later lived in Invergarry House. There are few descendants left of the MacDonells in the area and Jock is justly proud of the fact that his great, great grandfather slept on the hill with the chief of the MacDonells, in their plaids in the bracken, while out hunting deer. At that time they used deer hounds to bay the deer and Glengarry was almost the last estate to use this practice in hunting, although Jock thought that neighbouring Kylachy at Fort Augustus was in fact the very last one.

But Jock was full of stories having spent forty-five years as a ghillie on the river Garry. He taught many a one to fish through those years but maintains that women make the best fishers – they are not only more willing to listen but have a 'wonderful' light touch with the rod. His best fishing story doesn't involve himself but another ghillie, from Fort Augustus, who was in his prime when Jock was a wee boy.

The ghillie's name was Sandy MacGruer and he was out on Loch Ness one very cold windy wet day with a guest. The weather got worse and the guest took down the flaps of his deerstalker hat and tied them to further protect himself from the elements. He noticed Sandy failed to do this and was obviously feeling the cold. Eventually the guest asked Sandy why he hadn't tied the flaps on his hat, to which Sandy replied he hadn't done so since his accident. The guest was quite concerned at this and said how sorry he was but he hadn't heard of the ghillie's misfortune and wondered what had happened to him.

'It was a wild coarse day just like today and I took down the flaps of my deerstalker and tied them under my chin and when the guest offered me a dram I didn't hear him,' replied Sandy.

APRIL

The spiteful month

'April is the cruellest month', wrote T.S.Eliot when most other poets were being sentimental over the sense of sap and surge everywhere. Despite being described as that 'young iconoclast', T.S.Eliot knew that April's smiles could turn to tears.

Today, as I write, it has not snowed. For the past week we have had shivering, withering weather which has prolonged the struggle to reach the summit of this six month long winter. Perhaps it is the lambing storm. It certainly came designer-made to hit them hard; stinging sleet showers propelled by evil forces from the arctic north west, soaking their new earthly coats almost before the ewe had dried off the birth sac. The need to suck the precious colostrum has been more important than ever, the sharp snow showers sapping and dulling the urge to suck. The ewes have had to work twice as hard in the last week nursing their lambs, attending to every cry and finding secure shelter after every feed. One set of twins has had to have a booster bottle feed in the evenings as they were only just winning the struggle to survive as the wind's icy blade flashed around their hunched bony flanks. It has paid off for they now look less pinched and happier and are feeding more enthusiastically from their mum. Several gimmers had problems lambing but nothing more serious than a set of twins both of which presented with one leg back. Fortunately, having small hands I sorted this out successfully. Another beast almost beat me – and in front of an audience of mountain bikers as well. I was on my own and caught the distressed gimmer where I could which was on the edge of boggy ground. Once on the ground we rolled around together until I was certain she wouldn't get up and I could let go of her horn. Her birth presentation was perfect but not quite enough hooves showing to get a good grip to pull. So while I heaved and pulled the gimmer pushed and bellowed. I don't know whether the tourists knew what was happening or not as their line of sight was interrupted by some birches – but from the road the situation must have appeared very odd. However, the lamb was fine and the ewe accepted it immediately.

*   *   *   *

Both the collie and I suffered a degree of rough justice last week which left us licking our wounds and looking for sympathy. Nell's situation arose so quickly that she didn't know what had hit her until she was staring into the unblinking, vengeful eyes of a black-face ewe. The dog's dilemma started when, obeying my command to move the ewe and her lamb back into the field, the ewe ignored her. Moving slowly forwards, low to the ground, she approached the grazing ewe, who, stopping eating, changed her line of vision without moving her head, made eye contact with Nell and charged. She butted the collie unceremoniously down the bank, followed the attack through and a further brawl took place on flat ground before Nell came to her senses and her feet and fled round the house, away from the malevolent horns.

My experience was more protracted and embarrassing. I had been in Edinburgh staying with friends for a couple of days while attending the Court of the Lord Lyon. My kindly host had provided me with an omelette for supper which I duly ate and enjoyed. About lunchtime the next day I was gradually being overpowered by sleepiness and a thundering headache. Later on the train north, which was packed until Perth, the realisation dawned on me that I was going to be very sick. The journey proved disruptive for the person sitting next to me and eruptive for myself. Aviemore appeared like a port in the storm to my bloodshot eyes and for a further eight hours I continued to 'discharge'. My doctor diagnosed probable salmonella poisoning and it was only as the remaining strains of the dreaded lurgie were fading away some three days later that I smiled wryly at the subtlety of my rough justice. Here I am with forty fine hens who range through meadow and marsh, who scratch in burnished straw bales, who bathe fussily in dry, clean peat dust, who are fed on home grown golden oats which have never been sprayed or tampered with. They lay brown delectable eggs, with dark orange yolks containing lots of goodness and trace elements and no salmonella. But the first egg I eat away from the rarified atmosphere of my hen house strikes me down with satanic force from some fiendish virus.

My dear Nan

Rhubarb always reminds me of a dear departed neighbour, who, despite being dead sixteen years, I still miss. Perhaps it's because I still see the red roof of her house on the hill every morning as I fill my bucket for the hens at the outside tap. But rhubarb in particular makes me think of Nan. She had an exuberant patch not far from her stroup or outlet to her well and every year at this time made large quantities of rhubarb jam. Its delicate pinky sweetness was a delight and another world away from the coarse dull product I used to make.

But Nan had more sterling qualities than just jam making. She was open and honest and called a spade a spade. She would ask a question – many questions actually for she was fanatically interested in the small lives of this township — she would give an opinion and if that opinion offended or was near the bone, it didn't worry her; she never deceived, never patronised.

I used to love visiting her red tin roofed cottage called Baile-nan-craigean or the place of the frogs. Her house looked out on a miry pool which in summer was studded with tall yellow flags or irises, with their pale green sword-like leaves and amazingly complex flower heads. There was electricity in the house but no water and Nan retained a big open fire which, when I was a child, appeared like a magical sooty cave with a big black kettle bubbling and singing on the smokey hanging crook. She had a quaint silver sugar spoon on which was carved the name Alaska, and if I remember correctly, had many small figures apparently digging — perhaps they were gold diggers. But Nan was gone long before I had time to ask about the spoon.

Nothing was wasted at Baile-nan-craigean, every paper bag, jam jar, bottle, newspaper was saved. The *Radio Times* was especially precious for it was an ideal size for wrapping eggs in to protect them in the days before polystyrene containers were ever thought of. My pot of rhubarb jam was invariably put in a sugar bag — why should other people know our business. Every Sunday afternoon Nan walked to Inchdrein to visit her great friend, my aunt; other friends were called upon on other days. Time was put aside every week for visiting just as time was put aside for washing or ironing or helping the men in the fields. This practice of visiting has all but disappeared due in no small way to the insidious telephone.

My abiding memory of my old friend is one I know she would scold me for, in Gaelic, at that, for she was the last of the Strathspey Gaelic speakers in our township. I can see her in her rubber ankle boots, darned

stockings, a bag apron made out of meal sacks, wire curlers in her hair but with rosy red cheeks and brown twinkling eyes seeking my news, ready to give me hers.

The rhubarb still grows there but now in aimless abandon, the stroup gurgles, its daily song unchanged, but with never a white enamel pail to fill, the henhouse stands silent and empty, the rain trickling down the red drainpipe. Baile-nan-craigean is a jungle of nettles, a jumble of emotions.

Full circle

Spring work is progressing apace with the sowing of the oats and the spreading of fertiliser on the grass fields achieved this week. We've also sown grass seed along with the corn so that after harvest the field will return to permanent pasture. A pair of oystercatchers is nesting in the oat field this year and hopefully will hatch before the crows devastate their nest like last year. During cultivation we carefully marked the nest with a pile of stones to avoid destroying it with the machinery. In some EEC countries the government environmental agencies pay farmers who protect wading species which nest on their land. In many cases it is simply doing as we did and marking the nest with a pile of stones.

Talking of protecting birds – we've had to take measures to protect the newly sown oats from certain fowl. The hens have been imprisoned in a hen run but every luxury has been provided for them while the corn germinates. They have a large dust bathing area, a porcelain lined pool for drinking if you are a hen, for swimming if you are a duck, lots of broken straw bales to scratch in or recline on and newly lined laying boxes. There was dissension among the prisoners to start with when this new regime was introduced with the cockerels staging a rooftop protest. The dumpy hens wisely decided the barn roof was out of their flight range and settled for a cackle in a sunny corner.

Today as I write the temperature has soared to + 27C, appropriate, perhaps as today is Beltane or May Day. In days gone by this was an extremely important festival celebrated with bonfires on hilltops. To the Druids the sun was the centre of their divinity and fire, because of its affinity with the sun, was their mystic medium of worship. The bonfires were intended to appease the mysterious forces of nature, to ensure fertility in the soil, flock and herd and to purify the air of malign influences such as lightning, disease and above all, the power of witches.

As I washed my face in the Beltane dew this morning I heard a cuckoo 'cuckoo'.

MARINA DENNIS has lived all her life in the Highlands, being born in Inverness to parents from Lochaber. She lives in the foothills of the Cairngorms on a croft inherited from her aunt. Apart from croft work she writes a weekly column in the Inverness Courier and is a regular broadcaster on BBC Radio.